crochet
MONKEY
BUSINESS

CROCHET MONKEY BUSINESS
Copyright © TATSUMI PUBLISHING CO., LTD., 2010

First Published in the United States of America in 2013
by KP Craft, an imprint of F+W Media, Inc., 10151
Carver Road, Suite 200, Blue Ash, Ohio 45242.
(800) 289-0963. First Edition.

www.fwmedia.com

17 16 15 14 13   5 4 3 2 1

HOSHI MITSUKI NO TABISURU AMIGURUMI by Mitsuki Hoshi
Copyright © TATSUMI PUBLISHING CO., LTD., 2010
All rights reserved.
Original Japanese edition published by
Tatsumi Publishing Co., Ltd.

This English edition is published by arrangement with
Tatsumi Publishing Co., Ltd., Tokyo
through Tuttle-Mori Agency, Inc., Tokyo

English language rights, translation & production by
World Book Media, LLC
Email: info@worldbookmedia.com

Translator: Namiji Hatsuse
English Language Editor: Lindsay Fair
Designer: Lynne Yeamans

DISTRIBUTED IN CANADA BY FRASER DIRECT
100 Armstrong Avenue
Georgetown, ON, Canada L7G 5S4
Tel: (905) 877-4411

DISTRIBUTED IN THE U.K. AND EUROPE BY
F&W MEDIA INTERNATIONAL
Brunel House, Newton Abbot, Devon, TQ12 4PU, England
Tel: (+44) 1626 323200, Fax: (+44) 1626 323319
Email: enquiries@fwmedia.com

DISTRIBUTED IN AUSTRALIA BY CAPRICORN LINK
P.O. Box 704, S. Windsor NSW, 2756 Australia
Tel: (02) 4560 1600, Fax: (02) 4577 5288
Email: books@capricornlink.com.au

SRN: U8138
ISBN-13: 978-1-4402-33874-1

Cover designed by Geoffrey Raker
Manufactured in China

After learning to crochet from
a kit featuring her favorite
cartoon character, Mitsuki
Hoshi was inspired to start
a career as an amigurumi
designer. This self-taught
artist believes that everything
can be made out of yarn, from
animals to food. Mitsuki
lives in Japan, where she holds
classes regularly and is the
author of several craft books.
Her books have been translated
and published in many countries,
including the United States,
China, Taiwan, Thailand, France,
Sweden, and the Netherlands.
You can visit her web site at:
www.hoshi-mitsuki.com.

crochet MONKEY BUSINESS

a crochet story with
AMIGURUMI PROJECTS

mitsuki hoshi

CINCINNATI, OH

Contents

Meet Mockey, a lovable little monkey I first crocheted into life over 10 years ago. I found myself naming this little crochet monkey, and before I knew it, "Mockey the Monkey" had a full set of personality traits. His crew of friends followed, and a little amigurumi neighborhood came to life right under my crochet hooks!

Even when crocheting from a pattern, each amigurumi seems to have its own unique facial expressions and overall shape. I never know what my projects will look like until they are complete. I've also noticed that the little critters sometimes look like the person who crocheted them!

The aim of this book is to not only share these fun amigurumi projects, but to also illustrate the storybook whimsy they can inspire once you have crocheted some new friends of your own. They are guaranteed to inspire your creative world and bring out the kid in you.

Have fun and crochet!

— MITSUKI HOSHI

Meet Mockey
and
His Friends

Mockey is going on an adventure!

His friends next door wave goodbye as he departs on his big trip.
"Bon Voyage!"

INSTRUCTIONS:
Mockey p. 36,
Chicken and Chick p. 60,
Parrot p. 64

INSTRUCTIONS: **Panda** p. 68, **Ball** p. 104, **Strawberry** p. 105, **Basket** p. 106

For his first stop, Mockey visits his good friend Panda.

They spend the day playing fun games and enjoying delicious treats.

Mockey sets sail for his big adventure.

The salt air makes Mockey so hungry!
"Is that a real watermelon over there, or is it a mirage??"

Mockey's self-portraits

INSTRUCTIONS: **Life Preserver Ring** p. 107, **Banana** p. 108, **Watermelon** p. 109

Mockey arrives on exotic shores and makes a new friend!

Elephant welcomes Mockey with friendship beads.

INSTRUCTIONS: **Elephant** p. 72

Mockey meets a cute Koala named Kiki.

They spend the day just hanging out together.

INSTRUCTIONS: **Koala** p. 76

INSTRUCTIONS: **Tiger** p. 80

Mockey's next stop is with his old buddy Tiger.

Tiger and Mockey are best friends.

Mockey takes photos of the beautiful foliage.

He meets a squirrel who is busy gathering acorns.

INSTRUCTIONS: **Squirrel** p. 84, **Red Maple Leaf** p. 110, **Ginkgo Leaf** p. 110, **Acorn** p. 112, **Mushroom** p. 114

Mockey takes a knitting lesson from sheep.

A sweater will be perfect for the colder weather.

INSTRUCTIONS: **Sheep and Lamb** p. 88

INSTRUCTIONS: **Bear and Cub** p. 92

Mockey visits with the bear family.

They will start to hibernate soon. What nice little beds they have!
Mockey starts to miss his happy little home...

**Just outside,
reindeer wearing bells
stand in snow.**

They will be going on a trip
of their own very soon.

INSTRUCTIONS: **Reindeer** p. 96

Last stop home!

Snowman welcomes Mockey
back from his big adventure.

INSTRUCTIONS: **Snowman** p. 100, **Scarf** p. 111

Mockey settles into his cozy home for the winter.
Looking at his photos, he wonders....

Where to next?

Bears-To-Go

*"We can hit the road too!
Add a strap and
we're ready to travel."*

INSTRUCTIONS:
Bears-To-Go p. 116

Let's make mockey !

*"I hope you enjoyed meeting my friends, old and new.
Now I'll help you make some too."*

Tools and Materials

Use the following tools and materials to create a neighborhood of amigurumi:

Yarn

There's an astonishing range of yarn options out there today, but we'll mainly use 100% acrylic yarn, which comes in lots of fun colors. Mohair yarn, which is also available in acrylic blends, is recommended for making extra fluffy, cuddly textures—great for amigurumi. We will use a few different yarn weights. See below for more about yarn weight.

Crochet Hooks

Crochet hooks come in a variety of sizes. For the amigurumi in this book, you'll use sizes B/1 to E/4. A larger number indicates a thicker gauge hook. Generally, a bigger hook will be used with a heavier yarn. See below for more about hook size.

GAUGE

The three acorns pictured below were all made following the same pattern. However, different yarns and different crochet hooks were used for each acorn, which resulted in different finished sizes. For a larger finished size, use heavy yarn and a big hook. For a smaller finished size, use light yarn and a small hook. Keep gauge in mind, especially when making adult and baby versions of the same animal.

Yarns

DK-weight (#3 light) acrylic

Sport-weight (#2 fine) acrylic

Fingering-weight (#1 super fine) acrylic/wool blend

Fingering-weight (#1 super fine) 100% wool

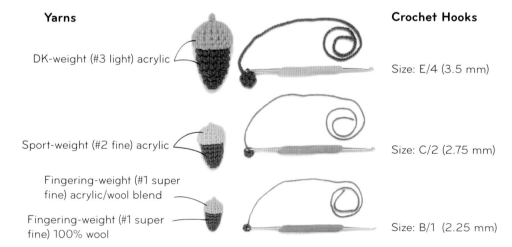

Crochet Hooks

Size: E/4 (3.5 mm)

Size: C/2 (2.75 mm)

Size: B/1 (2.25 mm)

Stuffing

Use cotton or polyester stuffing to fill and shape your amigurumi.

Stitch Marker

These are handy for keeping track of where a new row begins.

Eyes

There are many different eye options available at craft stores and online. Some are attached with glue, while others are fixed in place with a secure backing (these are called safety eyes). We'll use 4 mm, 6 mm and 10 mm sizes.

Glue

Quick-dry tacky glue is perfect for attaching eyes, felt, and other embellishments.

Toothpick

Very handy in making amigurumi! Use toothpicks for adding stuffing into small parts of an amigurumi (use the round end and not the sharp end).

Scissors

A small pair of scissors is essential for snipping yarn, embroidery floss, or little pieces of felt.

Yarn and Tapestry Needles

These are used with both embroidery floss and yarn for whipstitching parts together and also for embroidering details like noses and mouths.

Yarn and Embroidery Floss

Use for whipstitching amigurumi parts together and also for embroidering details like noses and mouths.

Amigurumi Stitch Guide

This guide provides an overview of the crochet stitch techniques and symbols used for the projects in this book. All the project instructions will reference visual patterns that use abbreviations and symbols. See page 54–55 for additional information on how to read the crochet patterns and charts.

Slip Knot

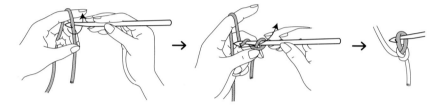

Make a loop. Insert the hook and pull the yarn through the loop to make the slip knot.

Slip Knot Ring (skr)

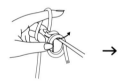
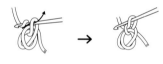

Wrap the yarn around the index finger twice

Slide the ring out and bring the yarn end to the front. Insert the hook in the ring and draw up the loop.

Yarn over, draw up the loop again, and tighten.

Yarn Over (yo): Wrap the yarn over the crochet hook.

Chain Stitch (ch)

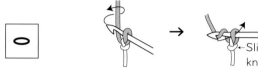 

Make a slip knot. Pull the yarn through the loop.

Pull the yarn through the loop again to make the next chain stitch.

Slip Stitch (sl st)

 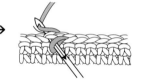 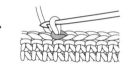

Insert the hook into the next stitch.

Yarn over.

Pull the yarn through the stitch and the loop already on the hook to complete the slip stitch.

Single Crochet (sc)

Insert the hook into the next stitch and yarn over.

Pull the yarn through the stitch.

Yarn over and pull the yarn through both loops on the hook.

One single crochet stitch is complete. Insert the hook into the next stitch to continue with single crochet.

Single Crochet Increase (inc)

This stitch will increase the number of single crochet stitches in a row by one.

 →  →  →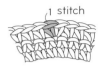

Make 1 single crochet.

Insert the hook into the same single crochet stitch (in previous diagram) and make another single crochet in this same stitch.

One single crochet increase is now complete.

Single Crochet Decrease (dec)

This stitch will decrease the number of single crochet stitches in a row by one.

 →  →

Insert the hook into the next stitch, yarn over, then pull the yarn through the stitch. Repeat process so you have 3 loops on the hook.

Yarn over and pull the yarn through all 3 loops.

One single crochet decrease is now complete.

Half Double Crochet (hdc)

Half Double Crochet Increase (hdc inc)

Double Crochet (dc)

Anatomy of an Amigurumi

Crochet the parts in the order noted by the numbers.

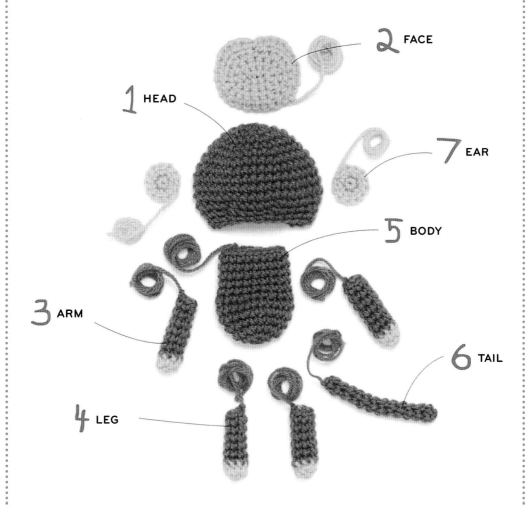

2 FACE

1 HEAD

7 EAR

5 BODY

3 ARM

6 TAIL

4 LEG

---

* In the photos at the beginning of the book, Mockey was made with dark brown yarn. In the photo above and the step by step photos on pages 36–53, we use a light brown yarn to make the stitches easier to see.

Step by Step Instructions for Mockey

Now let's try to make Mockey together. First you'll crochet the body parts in the suggested numerical order. Then, you'll assemble all the parts by whipstitching and adding embellishments.

The following directions will highlight the techniques and stitches you'll need for making each of Mockey's parts. These same techniques apply to all of the amigurumi in this book.

Crochet the Head

ROW 1: SLIP KNOT RING

This row will have 6 stitches made around an adjustable ring, noted here as the slip knot ring (skr). The slip knot ring functions as a drawstring, which means you can tighten the ring. This is great for crocheting amigurumi parts that will be filled with stuffing!

1 Start by making a slip knot ring (skr): Wrap the yarn around your index finger twice. Hold the yarn end between your index and middle fingers.

2 Insert the hook into the ring and pull the yarn through the loop and up.

3 Tighten the loop.

4 Repeat step 2.

5 Repeat step 3.

6 Pull the ring off your index finger. Hold the ring between your middle finger and thumb.

7 Insert the hook into the ring to begin a single crochet (sc) stitch. Yarn over (yo) and pull the yarn through the ring.

8 There will be two loops on the hook.

9 Yarn over (yo) and pull the yarn through both loops.

10 One single crochet
    (sc) stitch on the
    slip knot ring (skr) is
    complete.

11 Repeat steps 7–10
    to make another
    five single crochet
    (sc) stitches around
    the ring.

12 There will be six
    single crochet (sc)
    stitches total on the
    slip knot ring (skr).

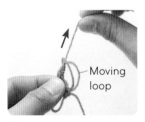

Moving
loop

Moving
loop

Yarn tail

13 Pull the yarn tail to
    make the stitches form
    a circle.

14 Find the loop that is
    able to move and pull
    to tighten.

15 Pull the yarn tail to close
    the gap between the
    first and last stitches

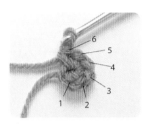

**I hope you made
a good slip knot ring...
I don't want stuffing
coming out of my head!**

16 Finish the row with a
slip stitch (sl st) into
the first stitch.

ROWS 2-11: INCREASING

Row 2 will have 12 stitches total. This means you will need to
make increases. To increase, make two single crochet stitches
into each of the six stitches of the first row: 2 x 6 = 12!

1 Insert the hook into the
first stitch of row 2.
Start to make a single
crochet (sc): Yarn over
(yo) and pull the yarn
through the stitch.

2 There will be two
loops on the hook.

3 Yarn over (yo) again
and pull the yarn
through both loops.

4 The first single crochet (sc) in the first stitch of row 2 is complete. This stitch is represented by the (☆).

5 Insert a stitch marker into the first single crochet (sc) stitch of row 2 (☆).

6 Make another single crochet (sc) into the first stitch.

7 The first single crochet increase (inc) is complete.

8 Following the same process, make two single crochet (sc) stitches into each of the next five stitches for a total of 12 stitches in row 2.

9 Remove the stitch marker and make the first single crochet (sc) stitch of row 3.

10 Reinsert the stitch marker into the first single crochet (sc) stitch of row 3. Follow the pattern and chart on page 58 to crochet rows 3-11.

ROWS 12-13: DECREASING

Row 12 will have 30 stitches and row 13 will have 24 stitches. This means that you'll need to decrease 6 stitches each row.

1 Start row 12 by making four single crochet (sc) stitches. To make a decrease in the fifth stitch, insert the hook into the next stitch, yarn over (yo), and pull the yarn through the stitch. There will be two loops on the hook.

2 Insert the hook into the next stitch, yarn over (yo), and pull the yarn through the stitch. There will be three loops on the hook now.

3 Yarn over and pull the yarn through all three loops.

4 One single crochet decrease (dec) is complete.

Am I done yet?!

ROW 14: SLIP STITCH

Continue crocheting up to row 14 of the head, following the pattern and chart on page 58. Make sure to use the stitch marker!

| After completing row 14, you'll make a slip stitch (sl st) to finish the head.

Lookin' good!

2 Insert the hook into the first stitch of row 14 (noted by stitch marker). Yarn over (yo) and pull the yarn through the stitch and the loop already on the hook.

3 The slip stitch (sl st) is complete. Yarn over (yo) and pull the yarn through the loop to make a knot. Cut the yarn, leaving an 8" (20 cm) long tail.

4 Pull the yarn tail to tighten the knot. The head is now complete.

Crochet the Face

ROWS 1-2: TURNING CHAINS

Turning chains are chain stitches often worked between rows to bring your yarn to the necessary height for working the next row.

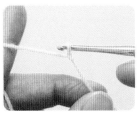

1 Start by making a slip knot (refer to the Amigurumi Stitch Guide on page 32).

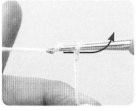

2 Yarn over (yo) and pull the yarn through the loop (this is not considered the first stitch).

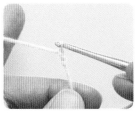

3 Make a chain stitch (ch). This is the first stitch.

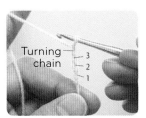

4 Make three more chain stitches (ch) for a total of four. The fourth chain stitch (ch) will be the turning chain.

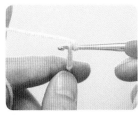

5 Insert the hook into the third chain stitch (ch).

6 Yarn over (yo) and pull the yarn through the stitch and the loop to complete one single crochet (sc) stitch.

7 Insert the stitch marker into the single crochet (sc) stitch you just completed.

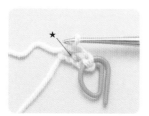

8 Make a single crochet (sc) stitch into each of the two remaining chain stitches (ch). The (★) indicates the first chain stitch (ch) you originally made.

9 Make another two single crochet (sc) stitches into the first chain stitch (ch) (★). This is a single crochet increase (inc).

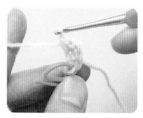

10 Turn the work so you are on the other side of the chain stitches (ch). Make another single crochet (sc) stitch into the first chain stitch (ch) (★). This makes a total of four stitches into the first chain stitch (ch) (★).

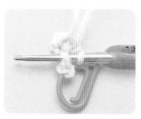

11 Make a single crochet (sc) stitch into each of the two remaining chain stitches (ch). Then make another two single crochet (sc) stitches into the last chain stitch (ch). This is a single crochet increase (inc).

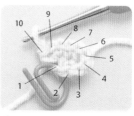

12 Count and make sure you have completed 10 stitches.

13 Insert the hook into the first stitch (noted by stitch marker) and make a slip stitch (sl st).

14 Row 1 is complete.

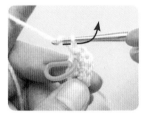

1 To start row 2, yarn over (yo) and pull the yarn through the loop to make one chain stitch (ch).

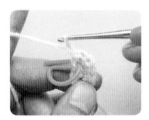

2 The chain stitch (ch) is complete.

3 Insert the hook into the first stitch (as noted by stitch marker). Make one single crochet (sc) stitch.

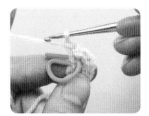

4 The first single crochet (sc) stitch of row 2 is complete.

5 Move the stitch marker to the first single crochet (sc) stitch on row 2 (the stitch you just completed).

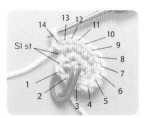

6 Follow the pattern and chart on page 57 to finish crocheting row 2. Count and make sure you have 14 stitches.

ROW 3: HALF DOUBLE CROCHET

Follow the pattern and chart on page 57 to start crocheting row 3. After making two single crochet increases, you'll need to make a half double crochet (hdc) stitch.

7 Insert the hook into the first stitch of row 2 (noted by stitch marker) and make a slip stitch (sl st) to complete row 2.

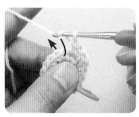

1 Yarn over (yo) and insert the hook into the next stitch.

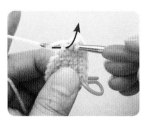

2 Yarn over (yo) and pull the yarn through the stitch.

3 There will be three loops on the hook.

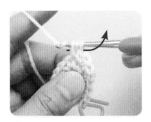

4 Pull the yarn through all three loops.

5 One half double crochet (hdc) stitch is complete.

To complete the face: Follow the pattern and chart on page 57. Finish the face the same way as the head.

Crochet the Arm or Leg

ROWS 2-3: CHANGING YARN COLORS
Work the first two rows of the arms and legs in beige, then switch to dark brown.

1 Follow the pattern and chart on page 59 to crochet rows 1-2. When making the last single crochet (sc) stitch of row 2, stop when there are two loops on the hook.

2 Yarn over (yo) using the new yarn color and pull the yarn through the loops.

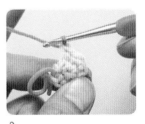

3 The yarn color change is now complete. Cut the first yarn color, leaving a tail a few inches long.

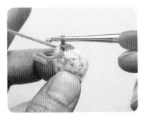

4 Insert the hook into the first stitch of row 2 (noted by stitch marker) and make a slip stitch (sl st) to complete row 2.

5 To start row 3, make one chain stitch (ch). Insert the hook into the first stitch (as noted by the stitch marker). Make one single crochet (sc) stitch.

6 Make six more single crochet (sc) stitches for a total of seven. Make a slip stitch (sl st) to complete row 3.

7 Follow the patterns and charts on page 59 to finish crocheting the arms and legs. Finish the legs in the same manner as the head, as shown on page 42.

Changing yarns leaves a yarn tail. Work over the yarn tail of the previous color, catching it as you work the new row with the new yarn color. This will secure the yarn tail and minimize its length. You can weave in any remaining yarn pieces later.

I love my yarn tail!

Finish Crocheting the Parts

Crochet the Body

Start the body in the same way as the head by making six single crochet (sc) stitches around a slip knot ring (skr). Tighten the loop and make a chain stitch (turning chain) before starting row 2. For the body, be sure to make one chain stitch (ch) between each row as a turning chain. This is noted in the body pattern on page 57. Follow the pattern to complete the body.

Crochet the Tail

Start the tail in the same way as the head by making six single single crochet (sc) stitches around a slip knot ring (skr). Tighten the loop and make a chain stitch (turning chain) before starting row 2. Crochet rows 2-13 as noted in the pattern and chart on page 57.

Crochet the Ears

Start each ear with a slip knot ring (skr). Make seven single crochet (sc) stitches around the ring. Tighten the loop and make a chain stitch (turning chain) before starting row 2. Crochet row 2 as noted in the pattern and chart on page 56.

Assemble the Parts

STUFF THE PARTS

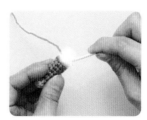

1 Insert stuffing inside the head, body, arms, legs, and tail.

2 Use the rounded end of a toothpick to stuff small parts, such as the arms and legs.

Toothpicks are perfect for stuffing my arms and legs!

PREPARE THE HEAD AND THE FACE

1 Thread the head yarn tail onto a yarn needle. Insert the needle through the stuffing and pull it out on the other side of the head.

2 Trim any excess yarn with scissors.

3 Thread one of the face yarn tails onto a yarn needle and draw it out on the other side. Trim any excess yarn with scissors.

ATTACH THE FACE TO THE HEAD

Whipstitch to attach the face to the head. The whipstitch is an overcast stitch used to join pieces together. This stitch is used to assemble all of the amigurumi in the book.

1 Thread the remaining face yarn tail onto a yarn needle. Begin whipstitching the face to the head by picking up a stitch on the head.

2 Insert the needle back through the face. Continue stitching through the head and face with close, even stitches.

3 After making the last stitch, insert the needle into the head and draw it out far away from the whipstitching. Trim the excess yarn.

ATTACH THE EYES

1 Apply a dab of glue to the back of each eye piece.

2 Adhere the eye pieces to the face (refer to page 59 for positioning).

I love to smile!

ATTACH THE MOUTH

Any time a project calls for embroidery, refer to the assembly diagram for the correct position. The assembly diagram for Mockey is on page 59. It notes to stitch the mouth onto the third row of the face. The mouth is made with red yarn, as noted on the project materials list on page 56.

1 Insert a threaded needle into the head and through the stuffing, drawing it out at the third row of the face.

2 Shape the mouth, then insert the needle back into the head at a point equal to step 1.

3 Add a dab of glue to adhere the mouth to the face. This will prevent the mouth from moving.

ATTACH THE HEAD TO THE BODY

I feel much better now that I have a good head on my shoulders!

1 Thread the body yarn tail onto a yarn needle. Whipstitch the head to the body.

2 After making the last stitch, insert the needle into the body and draw it out far away from the whip-stitching. Trim the excess yarn.

ATTACH THE ARMS AND LEGS TO THE BODY

1 Position the legs as noted the assembly diagram on page 59.

2 Thread the leg yarn tail onto a yarn needle. Whipstitch the leg to the body.

3 Repeat step 2 for the second leg.

ATTACH THE TAIL

5 Attach the arms following the same process used to attach the legs.

6 The arms and legs are now attached.

| Position the tail as noted in the assembly diagram on page 59. Thread the tail yarn tail onto a yarn needle. Whipstitch the tail to the body.

ATTACH THE EARS

All done!

| Position the ear as noted in the assembly diagram on page 59. Thread the ear yarn tail onto a yarn needle. Whip-stitch the ear to the head. Repeat for the other ear.

How to Use Crochet Patterns and Charts

In this book, the crochet instructions for each amigurumi include patterns and charts. The pattern contains symbols, while the chart uses numbers. Both versions contain the same information. The following guide shows how to read the patterns and charts used in this book.

Example of Pattern

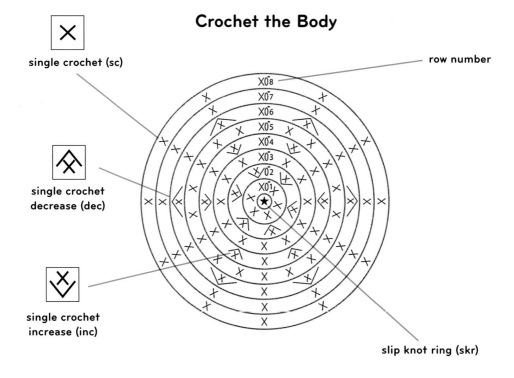

single crochet (sc)

single crochet decrease (dec)

single crochet increase (inc)

Crochet the Body

row number

slip knot ring (skr)

Example of Chart

the number of stitches to crochet per row

BODY

the number of the row

Row	Stitches
8	12
7	12
6	12
5	18
4	18
3	12
2	12
1	6

work even

(-6)

work even

(+6)

work even

(+6)

skr

negative numbers indicate decrease

crochet the same number of stitches as in the previous row

positive numbers indicate increase

slip knot ring
(refer to Amigurumi Stitch Guide on pages 32–34)

I love crochet patterns AND charts!

Mockey Shown on page 9

Materials

YARN

- 51 yards (13 g) of sport-weight (#2 fine) acrylic in dark brown

- 16 yards (4 g) of sport-weight (#2 fine) acrylic in beige

- Small amount of fingering-weight (#1 super fine) wool in red

NOTIONS

- Two 4 mm diameter eyes in black

- Stuffing

HOOK

- C/2 (2.75 mm)

How to Make

1. Crochet each part following the patterns and charts.

2. Stuff each part, except for the face and ears.

3. Whipstitch the face to the head.

4. Attach the eyes, following placement noted in the assembly diagram on page 59.

5. Embroider the mouth with the red yarn. Add a dab of glue to adhere the mouth to the face.

6. Whipstitch the head, arms, legs, and tail to the body.

7. Whipstitch the ears to the head.

Crochet the Ears

Attach this side to the head

EARS
(make 2)

Row	Stitches	
2	12	(+5)
1	7	skr

 = beige

Crochet the Face

Bottom

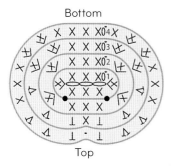

Top

⬤ = beige

● = Eye position

Use the wrong side of the sc as the outside fabric.

FACE

Row	Stitches	
4	30	
3	22	(+8 each row)
2	14	(+4)
1	10	ch 3

Crochet the Tail

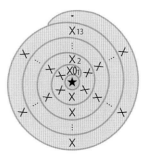

TAIL

Row	Stitches	
13	6	
|	|	work even
2	6	
1	6	skr

⬤ = dark brown

Crochet the Body

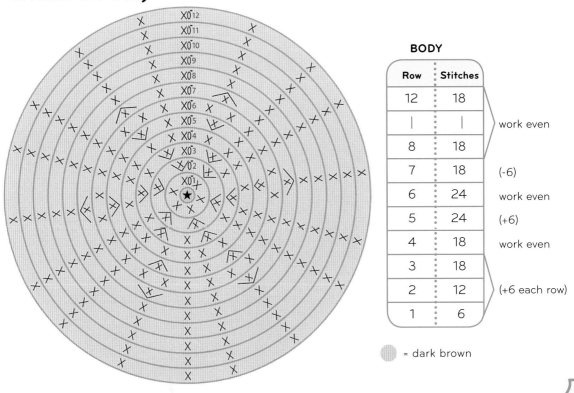

BODY

Row	Stitches	
12	18	
|	|	work even
8	18	
7	18	(-6)
6	24	work even
5	24	(+6)
4	18	work even
3	18	
2	12	(+6 each row)
1	6	

⬤ = dark brown

Crochet the Head

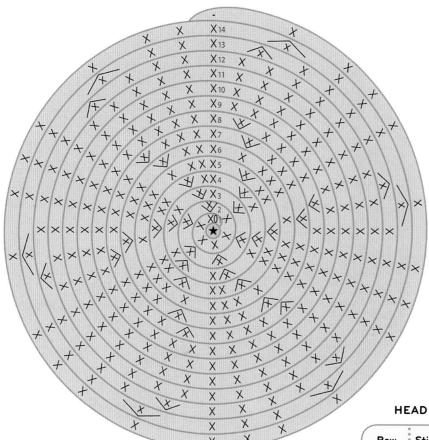

= dark brown

HEAD

Row	Stitches	
14	24	work even
13	24	(-6 each row)
12	30	
11	36	
|	|	work even
8	36	
7	36	(+6 each row)
6	30	
5	24	work even
4	24	(+6 each row)
3	18	
2	12	
1	6	skr

Crochet the Legs

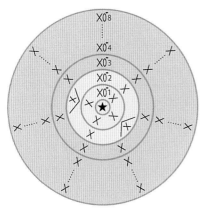

LEGS
(make 2)

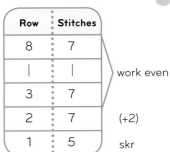

= beige

= dark brown

Row	Stitches	
8	7	work even
3	7	
2	7	(+2)
1	5	skr

Crochet the Arms

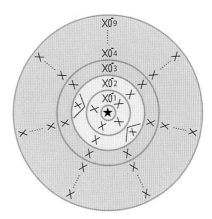

ARMS
(make 2)

Row	Stitches	
9	7	work even
3	7	
2	7	(+2)
1	5	skr

Assembly Diagram

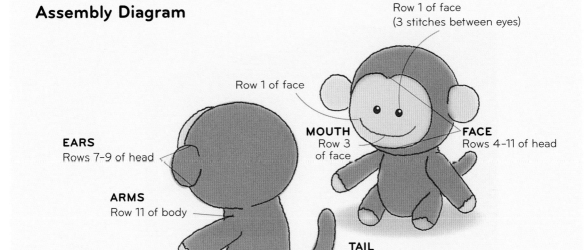

EYES
Row 1 of face
(3 stitches between eyes)

Row 1 of face

MOUTH
Row 3
of face

FACE
Rows 4–11 of head

EARS
Rows 7–9 of head

ARMS
Row 11 of body

LEGS
Rows 4–5 of body

TAIL
Rows 3–4 of body

Chicken and Chick Shown on pages 8–9

Materials

YARN

Chicken

- 31 yards (8 g) of sport-weight (#2 fine) acrylic in white
- 8 yards (2 g) of sport-weight (#2 fine) acrylic in yellow
- 8 yards (2 g) of sport-weight (#2 fine) acrylic in red

Chick

- 26 yards (6 g) of aran-weight (#4 medium) acrylic/mohair blend in yellow
- 8 yards (2 g) of sport-weight (#2 fine) acrylic in orange

NOTIONS

- Two 6 mm diameter eyes in black (chicken)
- Two 4 mm diameter eyes in black (chick)
- Stuffing

HOOKS

- B/1 (2.25 mm) (chick)
- C/2 (2.75 mm) (chicken)

How to Make

1. Crochet each part following the patterns and charts.

2. Stuff the head, body, and beak.

3. Attach the eyes. Whipstitch the beak and comb (for chicken only) to the head. Whipstitch the head to the body.

4. Fold the wings in half and whipstitch together.

5. Whipstitch the wings, legs, and tail to the body.

Crochet the Beak
(chicken and chick)

 = yellow (chicken) or orange (chick)

BEAK

Row	Stitches
1	10

ch 4

Use the wrong side of the sc as the outside fabric.

Crochet the Body
(chicken and chick)

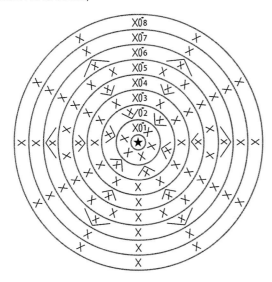

BODY

Row	Stitches	
8	12	work even
7	12	
6	12	(-6)
5	18	work even
4	18	(+6)
3	12	work even
2	12	(+6)
1	6	skr

◯ = white (chicken) or yellow (chick)

Crochet the Head
(chicken and chick)

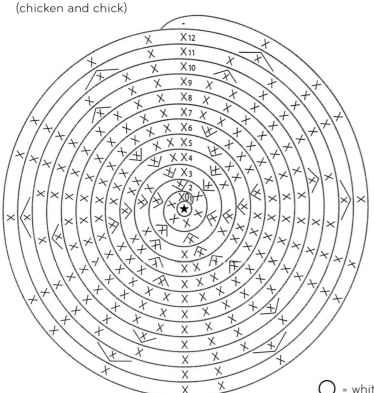

HEAD

Row	Stitches	
12	18	work even
11	18	(-6)
10	24	work even
9	24	(-6)
8	30	work even
7	30	
6	30	
5	30	
4	24	(+6 each row)
3	18	
2	12	
1	6	skr

◯ = white (chicken) or yellow (chick)

Crochet the Front and Back Combs
(chicken)

FRONT AND BACK COMBS
(make 2)

Row	Stitches	
2	5	work even
1	5	skr

 = red

Crochet the Legs
(chicken and chick)

LEGS
(make 2)

Row	Stitches	
2	6	work even
1	6	ch 2

● = yellow (chicken) or orange (chick)

Crochet the Wings
(chicken and chick)

WINGS
(make 2)

Row	Stitches	
3	18	(+6 each row)
2	12	
1	6	skr

○ = white (chicken) or yellow (chick)

Crochet the Center Comb
(chicken)

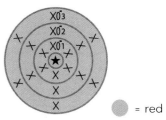

● = red

CENTER COMB

Row	Stitches	
3	6	work even
2	6	
1	6	skr

Crochet the Tail
(chicken and chick)

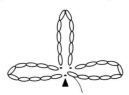

ch 10, sl st into first ch

Fold in half with right side facing out

Whipstitch together using yarn tail

Folded side

Assembly Diagram

CHICKEN

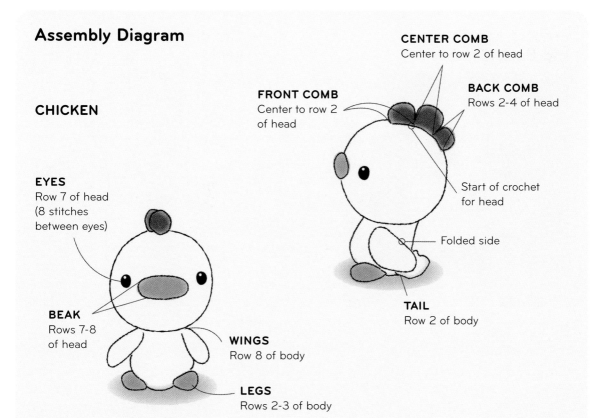

CENTER COMB
Center to row 2 of head

FRONT COMB
Center to row 2
of head

BACK COMB
Rows 2-4 of head

Start of crochet
for head

Folded side

TAIL
Row 2 of body

EYES
Row 7 of head
(8 stitches
between eyes)

BEAK
Rows 7-8
of head

WINGS
Row 8 of body

LEGS
Rows 2-3 of body

CHICK

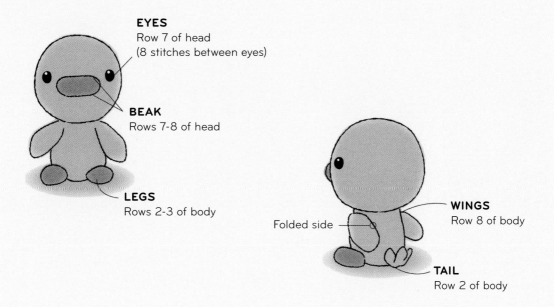

EYES
Row 7 of head
(8 stitches between eyes)

BEAK
Rows 7-8 of head

LEGS
Rows 2-3 of body

Folded side

WINGS
Row 8 of body

TAIL
Row 2 of body

Parrot <small>Shown on pages 8–9</small>

Materials

YARN

- 44 yards (11 g) of sport-weight (#2 fine) acrylic in white

- 12 yards (3 g) of sport-weight (#2 fine) acrylic in yellow

- 8 yards (2 g) of sport-weight (#2 fine) acrylic in beige

- 4 yards (1 g) of sport-weight (#2 fine) acrylic in orange

NOTIONS

- Two 6 mm diameter eyes in black

- Stuffing

HOOK

- C/2 (2.75 mm)

How to Make

1. Crochet each part following the patterns and charts.

2. Stuff the head, body, and legs.

3. Attach the eyes. Whipstitch the beak, cheeks, and comb to the head.

4. Pull the body yarn tail to close the opening. Secure and hide the yarn tail.

5. Whipstitch the head to the body.

6. Fold the wings in half and whipstitch together.

7. Whipstitch the wings, legs, and tail to the body.

Crochet the Cheeks

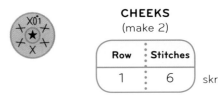

CHEEKS
(make 2)

Row	Stitches	
1	6	skr

 = orange

Use the wrong side of the sc as the outside fabric.

Crochet the Comb

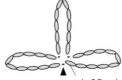

ch 10, sl st into first ch

 = yellow

Crochet the Tail

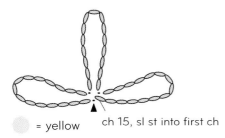

⬤ = yellow   ch 15, sl st into first ch

Crochet the Beak

BEAK

Row	Stitches	
2	6	work even
1	6	skr

⬤ = yellow

Crochet the Legs

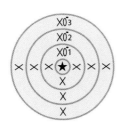

LEGS
(make 2)

Row	Stitches	
3	4	work even
2	4	
1	4	skr

⬤ = beige

Crochet the Wings

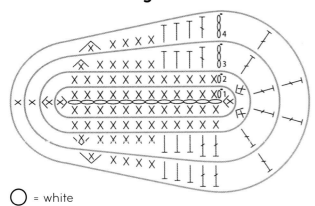

○ = white

WINGS
(make 2)

Row	Stitches	
4	25	(-2)
3	27	(-2)
2	29	(+1)
1	28	ch 12

WING

Attach this side to the chest

Fold in half and whipstitch together using yarn tail

End of crochet

Crochet the Body

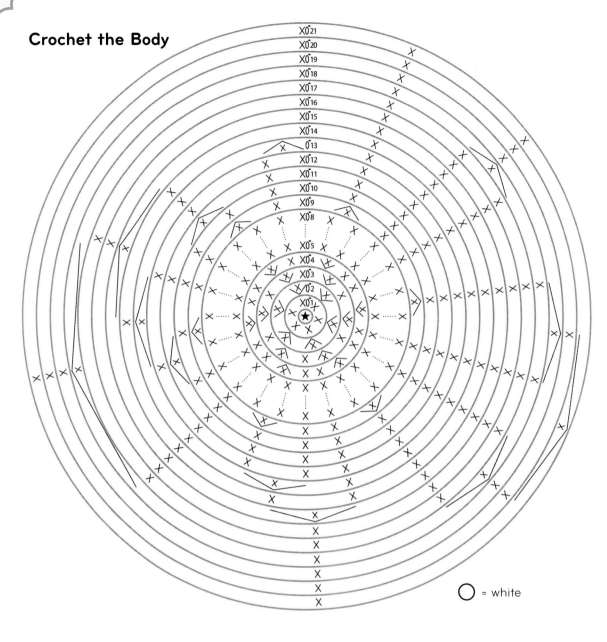

○ = white

BODY

Row	1	2	3	4	5	—	8	9	10	11	12	13	14	15	16	17	18	19	20	21
Stitches	6	12	18	24	24	—	24	18	18	16	16	13	13	11	11	11	8	7	7	6

skr

(+6 each row)

work even

(-6)

work even

(-2)

work even

(-3)

work even

(-2)

work even

(-3)

(-1)

work even

(-1)

Crochet the Head

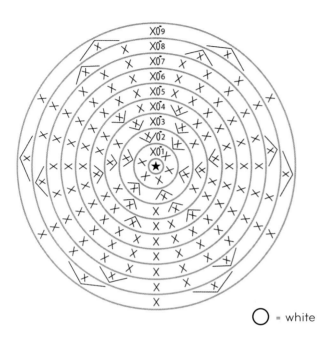

○ = white

HEAD

Row	Stitches	
9	12	(-6 each row)
8	18	
7	24	
6	24	work even
5	24	
4	24	
3	18	(+6 each row)
2	12	
1	6	skr

Assembly Diagram

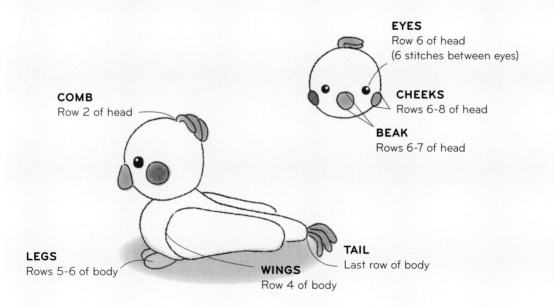

COMB
Row 2 of head

LEGS
Rows 5-6 of body

WINGS
Row 4 of body

TAIL
Last row of body

EYES
Row 6 of head
(6 stitches between eyes)

CHEEKS
Rows 6-8 of head

BEAK
Rows 6-7 of head

Panda
Shown on pages 10–11

Materials

YARN

- 31 yards (8 g) of sport-weight (#2 fine) acrylic in white

- 31 yards (8 g) of sport-weight (#2 fine) acrylic in black

- 4 yards (1 g) of fingering-weight (#1 super fine) wool in black

NOTIONS

- Two 10.5 mm diameter black and white eyes

- Embroidery floss in black (3 strands)

- Stuffing

- Glue

HOOKS

- B/1 (2.25 mm)

- C/2 (2.75 mm)

How to Make

1. Crochet each part following the patterns and charts. Use sport-weight yarn and a C/2 (2.75 mm) crochet hook for all parts, except for the nose. Use fingering-weight yarn and a B/1 (2.25 mm) crochet hook for the nose.

2. Stuff each part, except for the ears.

3. Apply dabs of glue to the back of the eyes and adhere to the eye patches.

4. Whipstitch the eye patches, nose, and ears to the head.

5. Embroider the mouth with the embroidery floss.

6. Whipstitch the head to the body.

7. Whipstitch the arms, legs, and tail to the body.

Crochet the Ears

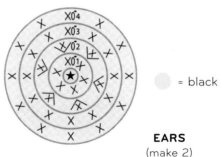

= black

EARS
(make 2)

Row	Stitches	
4	12	work even
3	12	
2	12	(+6)
1	6	skr

Crochet the Head

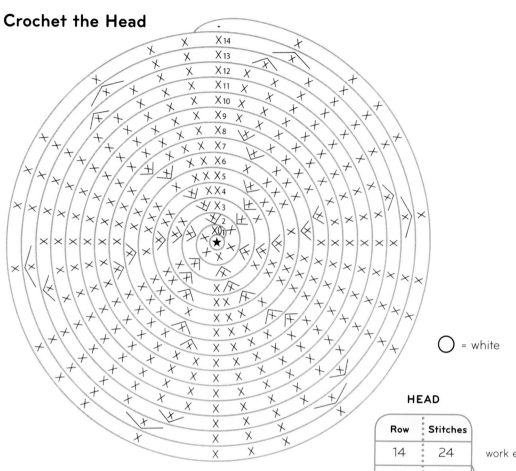

⭘ = white

HEAD

Row	Stitches	
14	24	work even
13	24	
12	30	(-6 each row)
11	36	
		work even
8	36	
7	36	
6	30	(+6 each row)
5	24	work even
4	24	
3	18	(+6 each row)
2	12	
1	6	skr

Crochet the Nose

NOSE

Row	Stitches	
2	6	work even
1	6	skr

● = black

Use fingering-weight yarn and B/1 (2.25 mm) crochet hook.

Use the wrong side of the sc as the outside fabric.

Crochet the Body

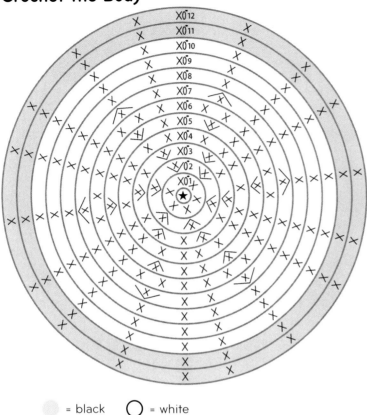

 = black ◯ = white

BODY

Row	Stitches	
12	18	work even
|	|	
8	18	
7	18	(-6)
6	24	work even
5	24	(+6)
4	18	work even
3	18	(+6 each row)
2	12	
1	6	skr

Crochet the Eye Patches

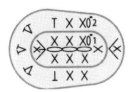

 = black

EYE PATCHES
(make 2)

Row	Stitches	
2	14	(+4)
1	10	ch 3

Use the wrong side of the sc as the outside fabric.

Crochet the Tail

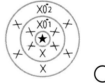

◯ = white

TAIL

Row	Stitches	
2	6	work even
1	6	skr

Crochet the Arms

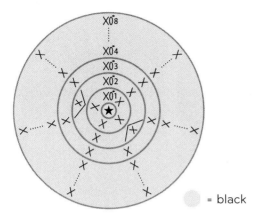

= black

ARMS (make 2)

Row	Stitches	
8	7	work even
3	7	
2	7	(+2)
1	5	skr

Crochet the Legs

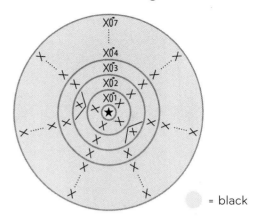

= black

LEGS (make 2)

Row	Stitches	
7	7	work even
3	7	
2	7	(+2)
1	5	skr

Assembly Diagram

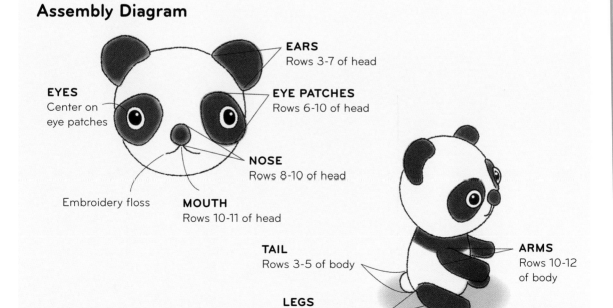

EARS
Rows 3-7 of head

EYES
Center on
eye patches

EYE PATCHES
Rows 6-10 of head

NOSE
Rows 8-10 of head

Embroidery floss

MOUTH
Rows 10-11 of head

TAIL
Rows 3-5 of body

LEGS
Rows 3-5 of body

ARMS
Rows 10-12
of body

Elephant Shown on pages 14–15

Materials

YARN

- 100 yards (27 g) of sport-weight (#2 fine) acrylic in gray
- Small amount of sport-weight (#2 fine) acrylic in red

NOTIONS

- Two 8 mm diameter eyes in black
- Stuffing

HOOK

- C/2 (2.75 mm)

How to Make

1. Crochet each part following the patterns and charts.

2. Stuff each part, except for the ears and tail.

3. Attach the eyes. Embroider the mouth with the red yarn. Add a dab of glue to adhere the mouth to the head.

4. Whipstitch the head to the body.

5. Fold the ears in half and whipstitch together.

6. Whipstitch the ears and trunk to the head.

7. Whipstitch the legs and tail to the body.

Crochet the Trunk

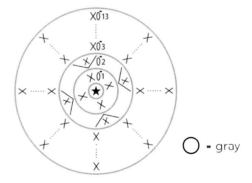

○ = gray

TRUNK

Row	Stitches	
13	8	
|	|	work even
3	8	
2	8	(+4)
1	4	skr

Crochet the Head

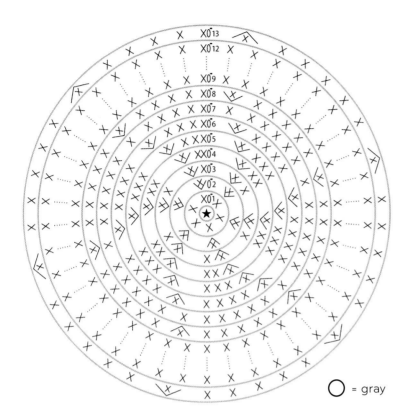

○ = gray

HEAD

Row	Stitches	
13	36	(-6)
12	42	
		work even
9	42	
8	42	(+6)
7	36	work even
6	36	
5	30	
4	24	(+6 each row)
3	18	
2	12	
1	6	skr

Crochet the Ears

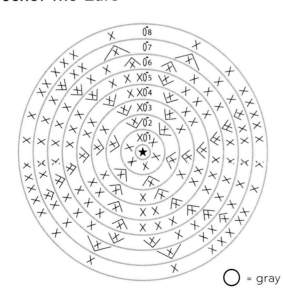

○ = gray

EARS
(make 2)

Row	Stitches	
8	30	
7	30	work even
6	30	
5	30	
4	24	
3	18	(+6 each row)
2	12	
1	6	skr

Crochet the Body

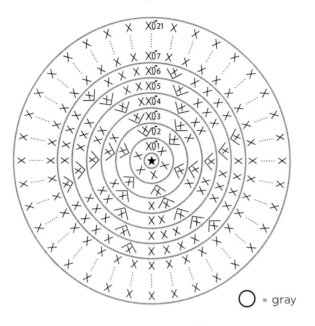

○ = gray

BODY

Row	Stitches	
21	36	work even
|	|	
7	36	
6	36	
5	30	
4	24	(+6 each row)
3	18	
2	12	
1	6	skr

Crochet the Legs

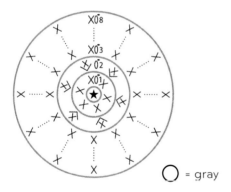

○ = gray

LEGS
(make 4)

Row	Stitches	
8	12	work even
|	|	
3	12	
2	12	(+6)
1	6	skr

Crochet the Tail

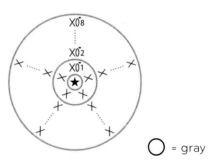

○ = gray

TAIL

Row	Stitches	
8	5	work even
|	|	
2	5	
1	5	skr

Assembly Diagram

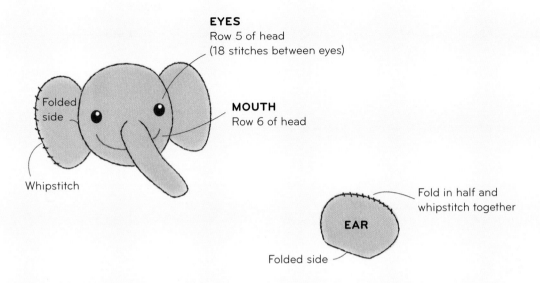

EYES
Row 5 of head
(18 stitches between eyes)

MOUTH
Row 6 of head

Folded side

Whipstitch

Fold in half and whipstitch together

EAR

Folded side

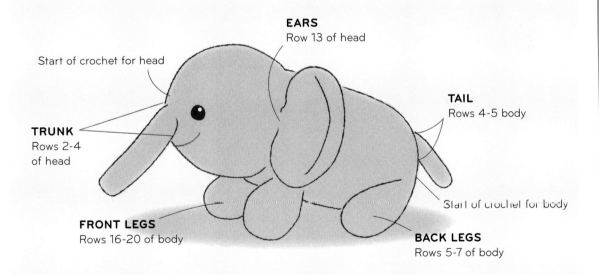

EARS
Row 13 of head

Start of crochet for head

TAIL
Rows 4-5 body

TRUNK
Rows 2-4
of head

Start of crochet for body

FRONT LEGS
Rows 16-20 of body

BACK LEGS
Rows 5-7 of body

Koala Shown on page 16

Materials

YARN

- 47 yards (12 g) of sport-weight (#2 fine) acrylic in gray

- 8 yards (2 g) of sport-weight (#2 fine) acrylic in black

- 6 yards (6 g) of worsted-weight (#4 medium) nylon chenille in white

- 9 yards (2 g) of fingering-weight (#1 super fine) acrylic/wool blend in pink

NOTIONS

- Two 6 mm diameter eyes in black

- Stuffing

HOOKS

- B/1 (2.25 mm)

- C/2 (2.75 mm)

- E/4 (3.5 mm)

How to Make

1. Crochet each part following the patterns and charts. Use sport-weight yarn and a C/2 (2.75 mm) crochet hook for all parts, except for the ears and bow. Use worsted-weight yarn and a E/4 (3.5 mm) crochet hook for the ears. Use fingering-weight yarn and a B/1 (2.25 mm) crochet hook for the bow.

2. Stuff each part, except for the ears and bow.

3. Attach the eyes. Whipstitch the nose, ears, and bow to the head.

4. Embroider the mouth with the black yarn. Add a dab of glue to adhere the mouth to the face.

5. Whipstitch the head to the body.

6. Whipstitch the arms, legs, and tail to the body.

Crochet the Nose

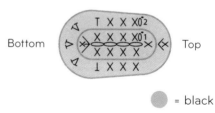

⬤ = black

NOSE

Row	Stitches	
2	16	(+4)
1	12	ch 4

Use the wrong side of the sc as the outside fabric.

Crochet the Legs

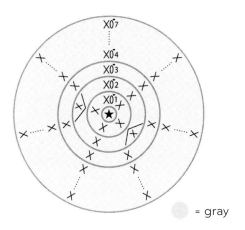

= gray

LEGS
(make 2)

Row	Stitches	
7	7	work even
3	7	
2	7	(+2)
1	5	skr

Crochet the Arms

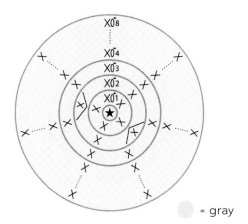

= gray

ARMS
(make 2)

Row	Stitches	
8	7	work even
3	7	
2	7	(+2)
1	5	skr

Crochet the Ears

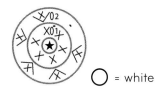

○ = white

EARS
(make 2)

Row	Stitches	
2	10	(+4)
1	6	skr

Use worsted-weight yarn and
E/4 (3.5 mm) crochet hook.

Crochet the Tail

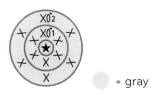

= gray

TAIL

Row	Stitches	
2	6	work even
1	6	skr

Crochet the Head

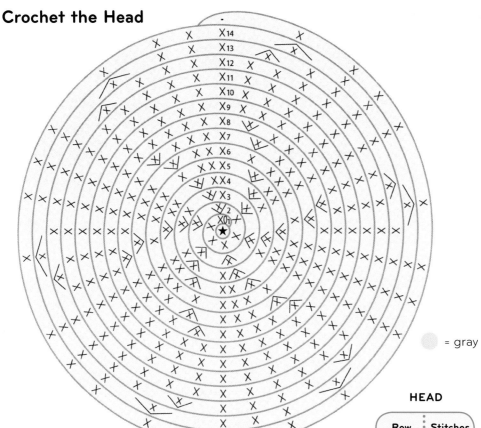

= gray

Crochet the Bow

ch 10, then work four rows of sc

◯ = pink

Crochet the Bow Center

→ 0X X X X X X X X X X X2
⟷ X X X X X X X X X X X01

chain 10, then work two rows of sc

◯ = pink

Use fingering-weight yarn and B/1 (2.25 mm) crochet hook.

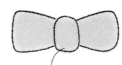

Wrap bow center around the bow and stitch short edges together at back.

HEAD

Row	Stitches	
14	24	work even
13	24	(-6 each row)
12	30	
11	36	work even
⏐	⏐	
8	36	
7	36	(+6 each row)
6	30	
5	24	work even
4	24	
3	18	(+6 each row)
2	12	
1	6	skr

Crochet the Body

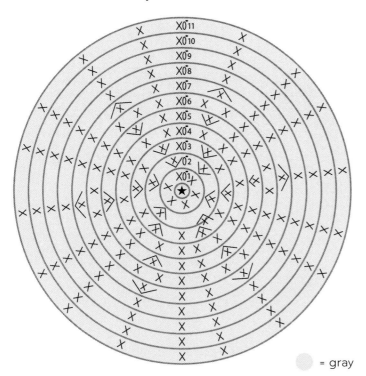

= gray

BODY

Row	Stitches	
11	18	
|	|	work even
8	18	
7	18	(-6)
6	24	work even
5	24	(+6)
4	18	work even
3	18	
2	12	(+6 each row)
1	6	skr

Assembly Diagram

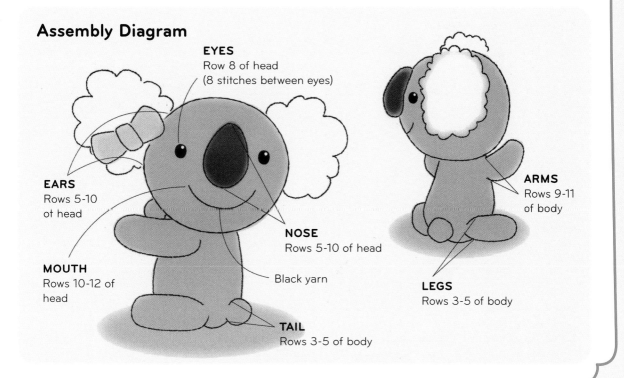

EYES
Row 8 of head
(8 stitches between eyes)

EARS
Rows 5-10
ot head

MOUTH
Rows 10-12 of
head

NOSE
Rows 5-10 of head

Black yarn

TAIL
Rows 3-5 of body

ARMS
Rows 9-11
of body

LEGS
Rows 3-5 of body

Tiger
Shown on page 17

Materials

YARN

- 47 yards (12 g) of sport-weight (#2 fine) acrylic in mustard yellow

- 20 yards (5 g) of sport-weight (#2 fine) acrylic in black

- 12 yards (3 g) of sport-weight (#2 fine) acrylic in white

- 4 yards (1 g) of fingering-weight (#1 super fine) wool in black

NOTIONS

- Two 6 mm diameter eyes in black

- Embroidery floss in black (3 strands)

- Stuffing

HOOKS

- B/1 (2.25 mm)

- C/2 (2.75 mm)

How to Make

1. Crochet each part following the patterns and charts. Use sport-weight yarn and a C/2 (2.75 mm) crochet hook for all parts, except for the nose. Use fingering-weight yarn and a B/1 (2.25 mm) crochet hook for the nose.

2. Stuff each part, except for the ears and tail.

3. Whipstitch the nose to the snout. Embroider the mouth with the embroidery floss.

4. Attach the eyes. Whipstitch the ears and snout to the head.

5. Embroider the stripes on the head.

6. Whipstitch the head to the body.

7. Whipstitch the arms, legs, and tail to the body.

Crochet the Ears

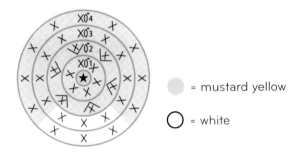

= mustard yellow

= white

EARS
(make 2)

Row	Stitches	
4	12	work even
3	12	
2	12	(+6)
1	6	skr

Crochet the Tail

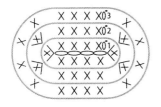

TAIL

Row	Stitches	
8	5	work even
|	|	
2	5	
1	5	skr

◯ = mustard yellow

● = black

Crochet the Snout

SNOUT

Row	Stitches	
3	16	work even
2	16	(+4)
1	12	ch 4

◯ = white

Use the wrong side of the sc
as the outside fabric.

Crochet the Nose

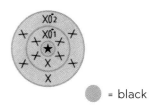

● = black

NOSE

Row	Stitches	
2	6	work even
1	6	skr

Use the wrong side of the sc
as the outside fabric.

Use fingering-weight yarn
and B/1 (2.25 mm) crochet
hook.

Crochet the Legs

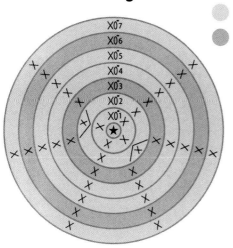

◯ = mustard yellow

● = black

LEGS
(make 2)

Row	Stitches	
7	7	work even
|	|	
3	7	
2	7	(+2)
1	5	skr

Crochet the Head

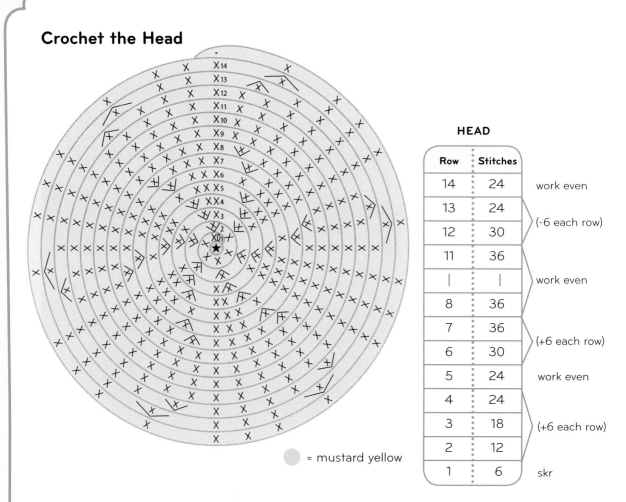

= mustard yellow

HEAD

Row	Stitches	
14	24	work even
13	24	(-6 each row)
12	30	
11	36	work even
|	|	
8	36	
7	36	(+6 each row)
6	30	
5	24	work even
4	24	(+6 each row)
3	18	
2	12	
1	6	skr

Crochet the Arms

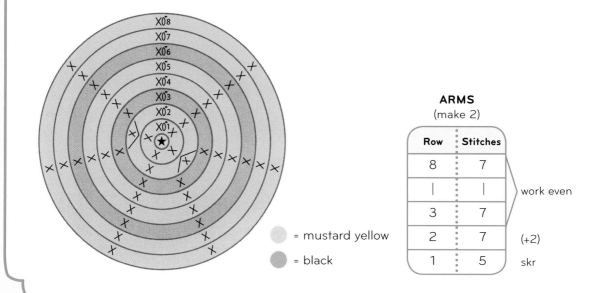

= mustard yellow

= black

ARMS
(make 2)

Row	Stitches	
8	7	
|	|	work even
3	7	
2	7	(+2)
1	5	skr

Crochet the Body

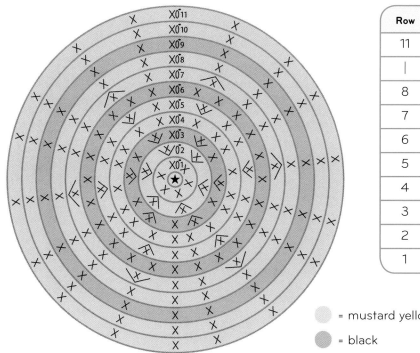

BODY

Row	Stitches	
11	18	work even
8	18	
7	18	(-6)
6	24	work even
5	24	(+6)
4	18	work even
3	18	(+6 each row)
2	12	
1	6	skr

◯ = mustard yellow

◯ = black

Assembly Diagram

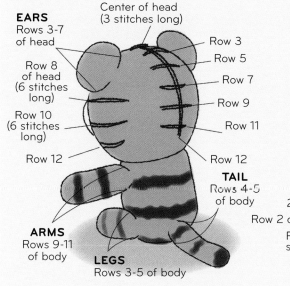

EARS
Rows 3-7
of head

Center of head
(3 stitches long)

Row 3
Row 5
Row 7
Row 9
Row 11

Row 8
of head
(6 stitches
long)

Row 10
(6 stitches
long)

Row 12

Row 12

TAIL
Rows 4-5
of body

ARMS
Rows 9-11
of body

LEGS
Rows 3-5 of body

For stripes on head, straight stitch with two strands of sport-weight yarn in black. Make stripes on back of head 5 stitches long and stripes on front of head 4 stitches long, unless otherwise noted.

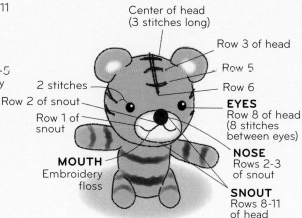

Center of head
(3 stitches long)

Row 3 of head

Row 5

Row 6

2 stitches

Row 2 of snout

Row 1 of
snout

EYES
Row 8 of head
(8 stitches
between eyes)

NOSE
Rows 2-3
of snout

MOUTH
Embroidery
floss

SNOUT
Rows 8-11
of head

Squirrel Shown on pages 18–19

Materials

YARN

- 70 yards (18 g) of sport-weight (#2 fine) acrylic in brown

- 12 yards (3 g) of sport-weight (#2 fine) acrylic in beige

- 8 yards (2 g) of sport-weight (#2 fine) acrylic in dark brown

- 4 yards (1 g) of fingering-weight (#1 super fine) wool in black

NOTIONS

- Two 6 mm diameter eyes in black

- Embroidery floss in black (3 strands)

- Stuffing

HOOKS

- B/1 (2.25 mm)

- C/2 (2.75 mm)

How to Make

1. Crochet each part following the patterns and charts. Use sport-weight yarn and a C/2 (2.75 mm) crochet hook for all parts, except for the nose. Use fingering-weight yarn and a B/1 (2.25 mm) crochet hook for the nose.

2. Stuff each part, except for the ears.

3. Whipstitch the nose to the snout. Embroider the mouth with the embroidery floss.

4. Attach the eyes. Whipstitch the snout, cheeks, and ears to the head.

5. Embroider the stripes on the head, body, and tail with the dark brown yarn.

6. Whipstitch the head to the body.

7. Whipstitch the arms, legs, and tail to the body.

Crochet the Ears

EARS
(make 2)

Row	Stitches	
3	6	work even
2	6	
1	6	skr

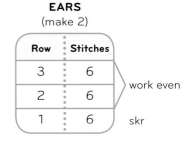

⬤ = brown

Crochet the Nose

NOSE

Row	Stitches	
2	6	work even
1	6	skr

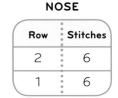

⬤ = black

Use the wrong side of the sc as the outside fabric.

Use fingering-weight yarn and B/1 (2.25 mm) crochet hook.

Crochet the Cheeks

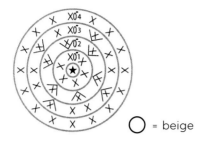

○ = beige

CHEEKS
(make 2)

Row	Stitches	
4	16	work even
3	16	(+4)
2	12	(+6)
1	6	skr

Crochet the Snout

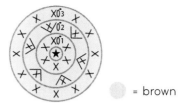

● = brown

SNOUT

Row	Stitches	
3	12	work even
2	12	(+6)
1	6	skr

Crochet the Legs

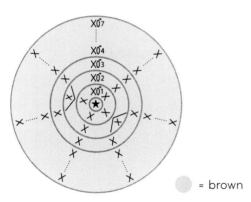

● = brown

LEGS
(make 2)

Row	Stitches	
7	7	
		work even
3	7	
2	7	(+2)
1	5	skr

Crochet the Arms

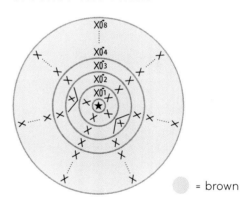

● = brown

ARMS
(make 2)

Row	Stitches	
8	7	
		work even
3	7	
2	7	(+2)
1	5	skr

Crochet the Head

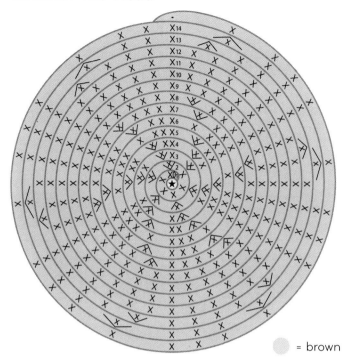

○ = brown

HEAD

Row	Stitches	
14	24	work even
13	24	(-6 each row)
12	30	
11	36	work even
|	|	
8	36	
7	36	(+6 each row)
6	30	
5	24	work even
4	24	(+6 each row)
3	18	
2	12	
1	6	skr

Crochet the Tail

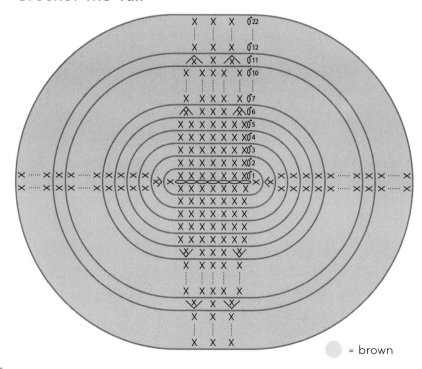

○ = brown

TAIL

Row	Stitches	
22	10	work even
|	|	
12	10	
11	10	(-4)
10	14	work even
|	|	
7	14	
6	14	(-4)
5	18	work even
|	|	
3	18	
2	18	(+2)
1	16	ch 7

Crochet the Body

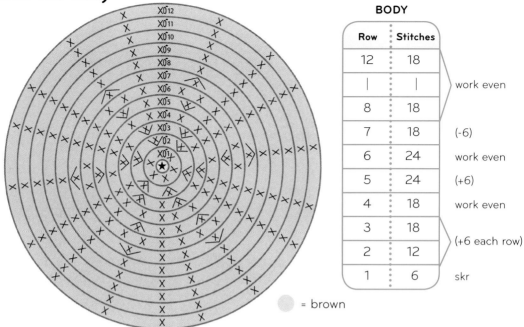

BODY

Row	Stitches	
12	18	
|	|	work even
8	18	
7	18	(-6)
6	24	work even
5	24	(+6)
4	18	work even
3	18	
2	12	(+6 each row)
1	6	skr

 = brown

Assembly Diagram

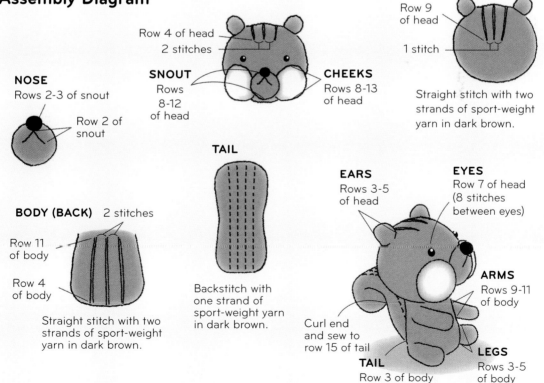

NOSE
Rows 2-3 of snout

Row 2 of snout

SNOUT
Rows 8-12 of head

Row 4 of head
2 stitches

CHEEKS
Rows 8-13 of head

Row 9 of head

1 stitch

Straight stitch with two strands of sport-weight yarn in dark brown.

TAIL

Backstitch with one strand of sport-weight yarn in dark brown.

BODY (BACK) 2 stitches

Row 11 of body

Row 4 of body

Straight stitch with two strands of sport-weight yarn in dark brown.

EARS
Rows 3-5 of head

EYES
Row 7 of head (8 stitches between eyes)

ARMS
Rows 9-11 of body

LEGS
Rows 3-5 of body

Curl end and sew to row 15 of tail

TAIL
Row 3 of body

Sheep and Lamb Shown on page 21

Materials

YARN

Sheep

- 30 yards (10 g) of DK-weight (#3 light) bouclé in white
- 27 yards (7 g) of sport-weight (#2 fine) acrylic in black
- Small amount of fingering-weight (#1 super fine) wool in white

Lamb

- 12 yards (4 g) of DK-weight (#3 light) bouclé in white
- 21 yards (5 g) of fingering-weight (#1 super fine) wool in black
- Small amount of fingering-weight (#1 super fine) wool in white

NOTIONS

- Two 9 mm diameter eyes in black and white (sheep)
- Two 6 mm diameter eyes in black and white (lamb)
- Embroidery floss in black (3 strands)
- Stuffing
- Glue

HOOKS

- B/1 (2.25 mm) (lamb)
- C/2 (2.75 mm) (sheep)
- E/4 (3.5 mm) (both)

How to Make

1. Crochet each part following the patterns and charts. Use a B/1 (2.25 mm) crochet hook for the lamb and a C/2 (2.75 mm) crochet hook for the sheep. Use fingering-weight wool for the lamb and sport-weight wool for the sheep for all parts, except for the body and head wool. Use DK-weight yarn and a E/4 (3.5 mm) crochet hook for the body and head wool of both the sheep and lamb.

2. Stuff each part, except for the ears.

3. Attach the eyes. Embroider the nose and mouth with the fingering-weight white yarn.

4. Fold the ears in half and whipstitch together. Whipstitch the ears and wool to the head.

5. Pull the body yarn tail to close the opening. Secure and hide the yarn tail.

6. Whipstitch the head and legs to the body.

Crochet the Ears
(sheep and lamb)

● = black

EARS
(make 2)

Row	Stitches	
3	12	work even
2	12	(+6)
1	6	skr

Crochet the Body
(sheep)

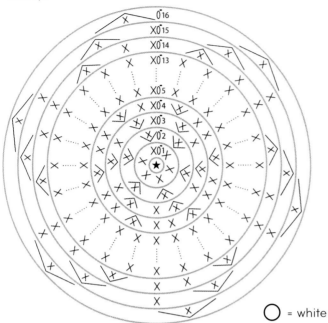

◯ = white

BODY
(sheep)

Row	Stitches	
16	6	
15	12	(-6 each row)
14	18	
13	24	
		work even
5	24	
4	24	
3	18	(+6 each row)
2	12	
1	6	skr

Crochet the Body
(lamb)

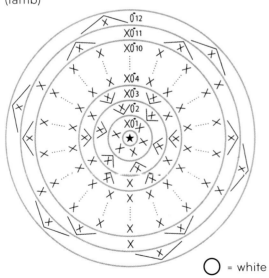

◯ = white

BODY
(lamb)

Row	Stitches	
12	6	
11	12	(-6 each row)
10	18	
		work even
4	18	
3	18	
2	12	(+6 each row)
1	6	skr

Use the wrong side of the sc as the outside fabric for both the sheep and lamb.

Use DK-weight yarn and E/4 (3.5 mm) crochet hook for both the sheep and lamb.

Crochet the Head Wool
(sheep)

Use the wrong side of the sc as the outside fabric.

Use DK-weight yarn and E/4 (3.5 mm) crochet hook.

$\bigcirc$ = white

HEAD WOOL
(sheep)

Row	Stitches	
3	18	(+6 each row)
2	12	
1	6	skr

Crochet the Legs
(sheep and lamb)

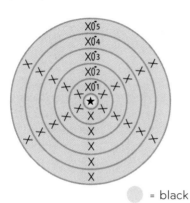

$\bigcirc$ = black

LEGS
(make 4)

Row	Stitches	
5	6	work even
|	|	
2	6	
1	6	skr

Crochet the Head
(sheep and lamb)

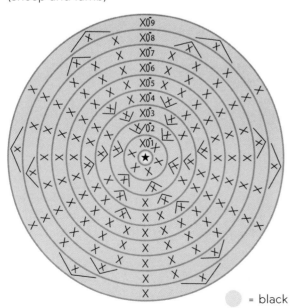

$\bigcirc$ = black

HEAD

Row	Stitches	
9	12	(-6 each row)
8	18	
7	24	
6	24	work even
5	24	
4	24	
3	18	(+6 each row)
2	12	
1	6	skr

Crochet the Head Wool
(lamb)

Use the wrong side of the sc as the outside fabric.

Use DK-weight yarn and E/4 (3.5 mm) crochet hook.

⭕ = white

HEAD WOOL
(lamb)

Row	Stitches	
2	12	(+6)
1	6	skr

Assembly Diagram

LAMB

EARS
Fold in half
Row 5 of head

EYES
Row 3 of head

NOSE AND MOUTH
(sheep and lamb)
Row 1 of head
Row 2 of head
Row 4 of head

BACK LEGS
Rows 9-10 of body

FRONT LEGS
Rows 4-5 of body

HEAD WOOL
(sheep and lamb)
Rows 2-7 of head

EARS
Fold in half
Row 6 of head

Folded side

SHEEP

EYES
Row 4 of head

Start of crochet for body

HEAD
(sheep and lamb)
Rows 1-3 of body

FRONT LEGS
Rows 4-5 of body

BACK LEGS
Rows 12-13 of body

Bear and Cub Shown on page 22

Materials

YARN

Bear

- 58 yards (15 g) of sport-weight (#2 fine) acrylic in reddish brown

- 15 yards (4 g) of sport-weight (#2 fine) acrylic in white

- 4 yards (1 g) of fingering-weight (#1 super fine) wool in black

Cub

- 42 yards (10 g) of fingering-weight (#1 super fine) wool in reddish brown

- 12 yards (3 g) of fingering-weight (#1 super fine) wool in white

- 4 yards (1 g) of fingering-weight (#1 super fine) wool in black

NOTIONS

- Two 6 mm in diameter eyes in black (bear)

- Two 4 mm in diameter eyes in black (cub)

- Embroidery floss in black (3 strands)

- Stuffing

HOOKS

- B/1 (2.25 mm) (bear and cub)

- C/2 (2.75 mm) (bear)

How to Make

1. Crochet each part following the patterns and charts. For the bear, use sport-weight yarn and a C/2 (2.75 mm) crochet hook for all parts, except for the nose. For the cub, use fingering-weight yarn and a B/1 (2.25 mm) crochet hook for all parts.

2. Stuff each part, except for the ears.

3. Whipstitch the nose to the snout. Embroider the mouth with the embroidery floss.

4. Attach the eyes. Whipstitch the snout and ears to the head.

5. Whipstitch the head to the body.

6. Whipstitch the arms, legs, and tail to the body.

Crochet the Tail
(bear and cub)

= reddish brown

TAIL

Row	Stitches	
2	6	work even
1	6	skr

Crochet the Nose

Use fingering-weight yarn and B/1 (2.25 mm) crochet hook for both the bear and cub.

Use the wrong side of the sc as the outside fabric for both the bear and cub.

(bear)

● = black

NOSE
(bear)

Row	Stitches	
2	6	work even
1	6	skr

(cub)

● = black

NOSE
(cub)

Row	Stitches	
1	5	skr

Crochet the Head
(bear and cub)

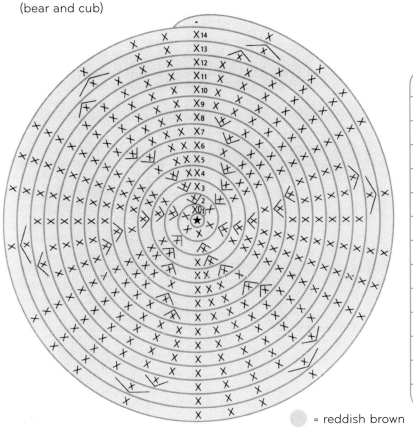

● = reddish brown

HEAD

Row	Stitches	
14	24	work even
13	24	(-6 each row)
12	30	
11	36	
ǀ	ǀ	work even
8	36	
7	36	(+6 each row)
6	30	
5	24	work even
4	24	
3	18	(+6 each row)
2	12	
1	6	skr

Crochet the Ears
(bear and cub)

EARS
(make 2)

Row	Stitches	
4	12	work even
3	12	
2	12	(+6)
1	6	skr

⬤ = reddish brown

Crochet the Snout
(bear and cub)

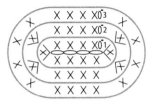

◯ = white

SNOUT

Row	Stitches	
3	16	work even
2	16	(+4)
1	12	ch 4

Use the wrong side of the sc as the outside fabric.

Crochet the Body
(bear and cub)

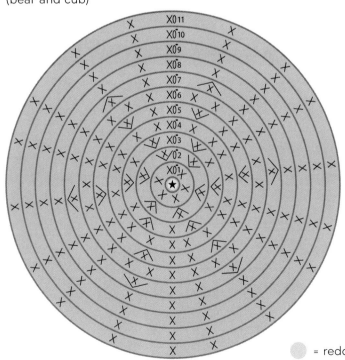

BODY

Row	Stitches	
11	18	work even
|	|	
8	18	
7	18	(-6)
6	24	work even
5	24	(+6)
4	18	work even
3	18	(+6 each row)
2	12	
1	6	skr

⬤ = reddish brown

Crochet the Arms
(bear and cub)

Crochet the Legs
(bear and cub)

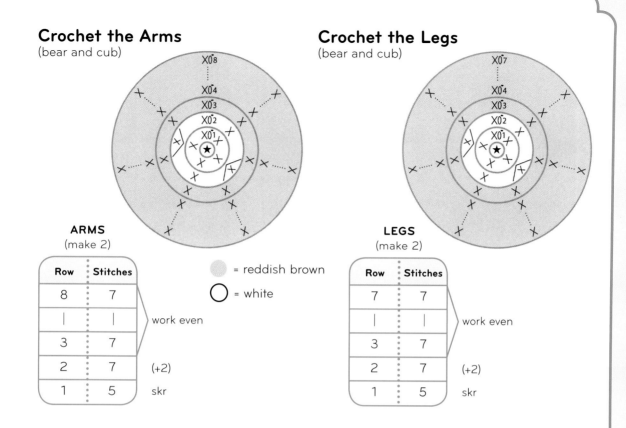

= reddish brown

⭕ = white

ARMS
(make 2)

Row	Stitches	
8	7	
|	|	work even
3	7	
2	7	(+2)
1	5	skr

LEGS
(make 2)

Row	Stitches	
7	7	
|	|	work even
3	7	
2	7	(+2)
1	5	skr

Assembly Diagram
Body part placement is the same for both the bear and cub.

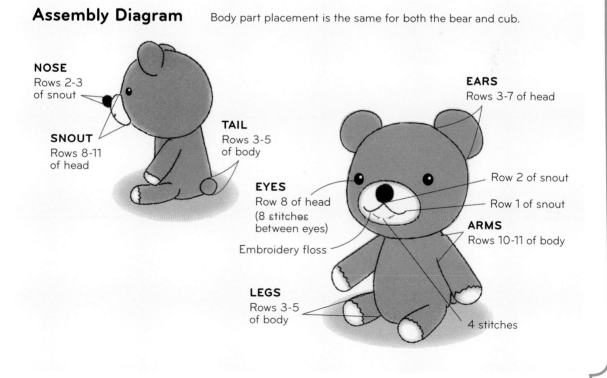

NOSE
Rows 2-3
of snout

SNOUT
Rows 8-11
of head

TAIL
Rows 3-5
of body

EYES
Row 8 of head
(8 stitches
between eyes)

Embroidery floss

LEGS
Rows 3-5
of body

EARS
Rows 3-7 of head

Row 2 of snout

Row 1 of snout

ARMS
Rows 10-11 of body

4 stitches

Reindeer Shown on page 23

Materials

YARN
- 78 yards (20 g) of sport-weight (#2 fine) acrylic in brown
- 20 yards (5 g) of sport-weight (#2 fine) acrylic in beige
- 4 yards (1 g) of sport-weight (#2 fine) acrylic in red

NOTIONS
- Two 8 mm diameter eyes in black
- One 1" (2.5 cm) long bell
- Ribbon
- Stuffing

HOOK
- C/2 (2.75 mm)

How to Make

1. Crochet each part following the patterns and charts.
2. Stuff each part, except for the ears.
3. Attach the eyes.
4. Whipstitch the nose to the snout. Embroider the mouth with the red yarn. Apply a dab of glue to adhere the mouth to the snout.
5. Fold the ears in half and whipstitch to the head. Whipstitch each short antler to a long antler. Whipstitch the snout and antlers to the head.
6. Pull the body yarn tail to close the opening. Secure and hide the yarn tail.
7. Whipstitch the head, legs, and tail to the body.
8. Tie the ribbon in a bow. Glue the bell to the bow, then glue the bow to the body.

Crochet the Nose

NOSE

Row	Stitches	
2	6	work even
1	6	skr

⬤ = red

Use the wrong side of the sc as the outside fabric.

Crochet the Ears

EARS
(make 2)

Row	Stitches	
3	12	work even
2	12	(+6)
1	6	skr

⬤ = brown

Crochet the Snout

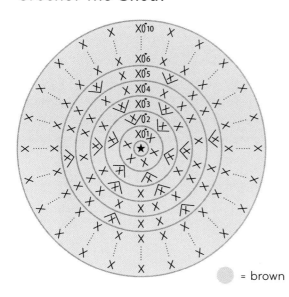

SNOUT

Row	Stitches	
10	24	
|	|	work even
6	24	
5	24	(+6)
4	18	work even
3	18	(+6 each row)
2	12	
1	6	skr

= brown

Crochet the Head

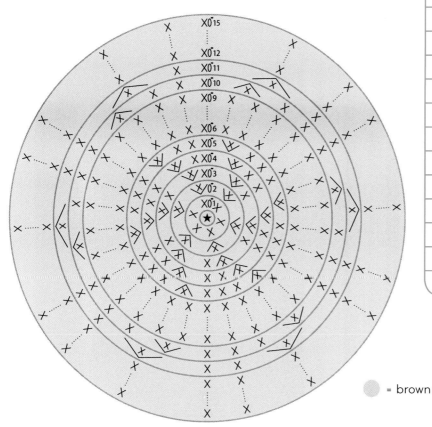

HEAD

Row	Stitches	
15	18	
|	|	work even
12	18	
11	18	(-6 each row)
10	24	
9	30	
|	|	work even
6	30	
5	30	
4	24	(+6 each row)
3	18	
2	12	
1	6	skr

= brown

Crochet the Tail

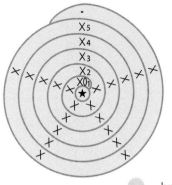

TAIL

⬤ = brown

Row	Stitches	
5	5	work even
|	|	
2	5	
1	5	skr

Crochet the Legs

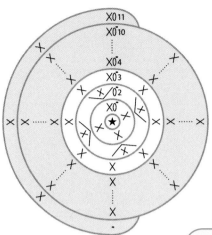

⬤ = brown

◯ = beige

LEGS
(make 4)

Row	Stitches	
11	4	(-4)
10	8	
|	|	work even
3	8	
2	8	(+4)
1	4	skr

Crochet the Body

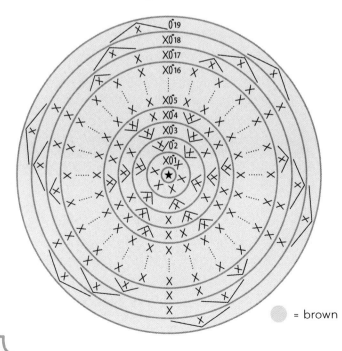

⬤ = brown

BODY

Row	Stitches	
19	6	
18	12	(-6 each row)
17	18	
16	24	
|	|	work even
5	24	
4	24	
3	18	(+6 each row)
2	12	
1	6	skr

Crochet the Long Antlers

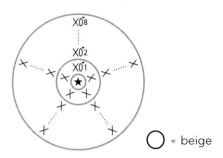

◯ = beige

LONG ANTLERS
(make 2)

Row	Stitches	
8	5	
|	|	work even
2	5	
1	5	skr

Crochet the Short Antlers

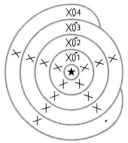

◯ = beige

SHORT ANTLERS
(make 2)

Row	Stitches	
4	3	(-2)
3	5	
2	5	work even
1	5	skr

Assembly Diagram

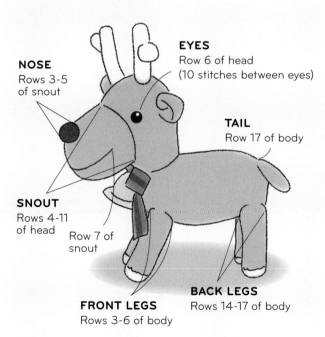

NOSE
Rows 3-5
of snout

SNOUT
Rows 4-11
of head

Row 7 of
snout

FRONT LEGS
Rows 3-6 of body

EYES
Row 6 of head
(10 stitches between eyes)

TAIL
Row 17 of body

BACK LEGS
Rows 14-17 of body

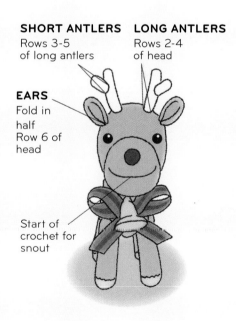

SHORT ANTLERS
Rows 3-5
of long antlers

LONG ANTLERS
Rows 2-4
of head

EARS
Fold in
half
Row 6 of
head

Start of
crochet for
snout

Snowman Shown on page 24

Materials

YARN

- 87 yards (20 g) of aran-weight (#4 medium) acrylic/mohair blend in white

- 15 yards (4 g) of sport-weight (#2 fine) acrylic in blue

- 8 yards (2 g) of sport-weight (#2 fine) acrylic in orange

- Small amount of fingering-weight (#1 super fine) wool in black

NOTIONS

- Two 6 mm diameter eyes in black

- Small piece of felt in yellow

- Stuffing

HOOK

- C/2 (2.75 mm)

How to Make

1. Crochet each part following the patterns and charts. Use two strands of aran-weight yarn for the head and body.

2. Stuff each part.

3. Attach the eyes. Whipstitch the nose and hat to the head.

4. Embroider the mouth with the black yarn. Apply a dab of glue to adhere the mouth to the head.

5. Whipstitch the head to the body.

6. To make the buttons, cut two 1/2" (1.3 cm) diameter circles from the yellow felt. Embroider an "X" onto each circle using the orange yarn, then glue to the body.

Crochet the Nose

 = orange

NOSE

Row	Stitches	
3	7	(+2)
2	5	work even
1	5	skr

Crochet the Hat

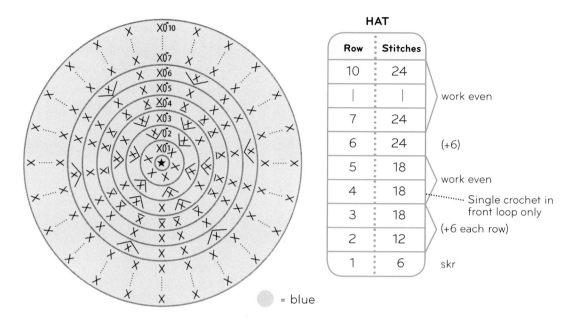

HAT

Row	Stitches	
10	24	
|	|	work even
7	24	
6	24	(+6)
5	18	
4	18	work even
3	18	Single crochet in front loop only
2	12	(+6 each row)
1	6	skr

⬤ = blue

Crochet the Head

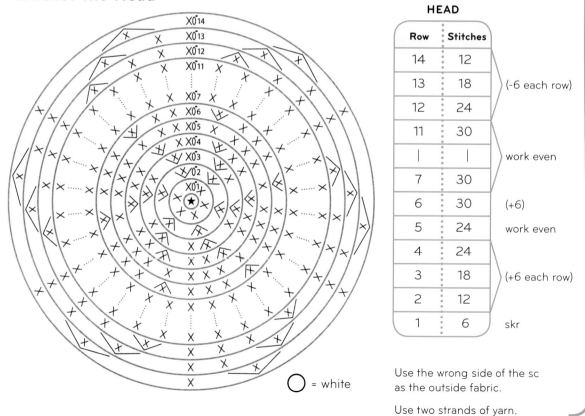

HEAD

Row	Stitches	
14	12	
13	18	(-6 each row)
12	24	
11	30	
|	|	work even
7	30	
6	30	(+6)
5	24	work even
4	24	
3	18	(+6 each row)
2	12	
1	6	skr

◯ = white

Use the wrong side of the sc as the outside fabric.

Use two strands of yarn.

Crochet the Body

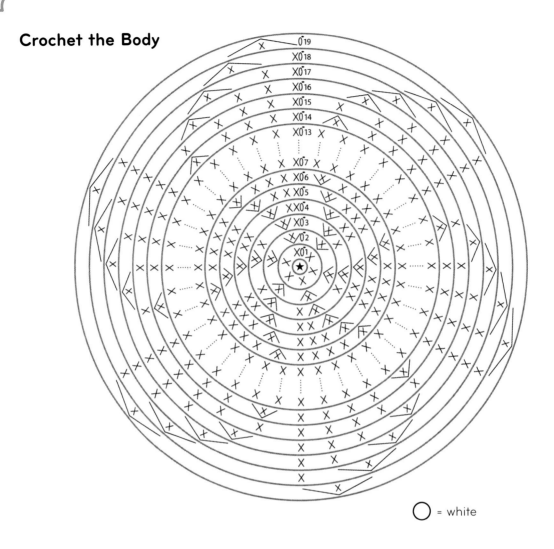

$\bigcirc$ = white

BODY

Row	1	2	3	4	5	6	7	—	13	14	15	16	17	18	19
Stitches	6	12	18	24	30	36	36	—	36	30	30	24	18	12	6

skr

(+6 each row)

work even

(-6)

work even

(-6 each row)

Use the wrong side of the sc as the outside fabric.

Use two strands of yarn.

Assembly Diagram

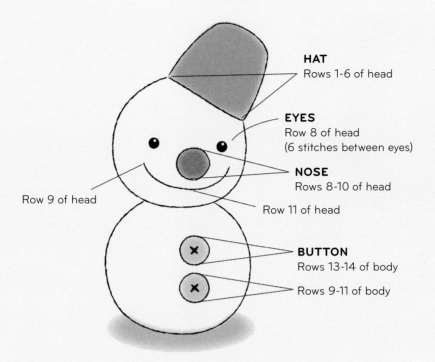

HAT
Rows 1-6 of head

EYES
Row 8 of head
(6 stitches between eyes)

NOSE
Rows 8-10 of head

Row 11 of head

Row 9 of head

BUTTON
Rows 13-14 of body

Rows 9-11 of body

Ball <small>Shown on page 10</small>

Materials

YARN

- 9 yards (2 g) of fingering-weight (#1 super fine) acrylic/wool blend in white

- 9 yards (2 g) of fingering-weight (#1 super fine) acrylic/wool blend in light blue

- 9 yards (2 g) of fingering-weight (#1 super fine) acrylic/wool blend in pink

NOTIONS

- Stuffing

HOOK

- B/1 (2.25 mm)

How to Make

1. Crochet the ball following the pattern and chart.

2. Stuff. Pull the ball yarn tail to close the opening. Secure and hide the yarn tail.

Crochet the Ball

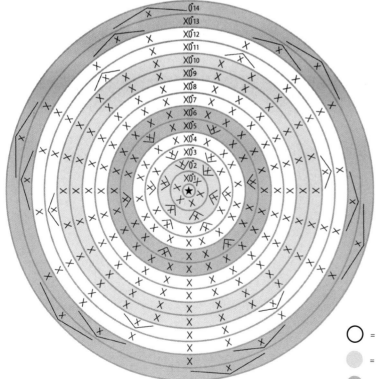

BALL

Row	Stitches	
14	6	(-6 each row)
13	12	
12	18	work even
11	18	(-6)
10	24	
		work even
6	24	
5	24	(+6)
4	18	work even
3	18	(+6 each row)
2	12	
1	6	skr

◯ = white

◯ = light blue

● = pink

Strawberry Shown on page 11

Materials

YARN

- 13 yards (3 g) of fingering-weight (#1 super fine) acrylic/wool blend in red

- 9 yards (2 g) of fingering-weight (#1 super fine) acrylic/wool blend in green

- Small amount of fingering-weight (#1 super fine) acrylic/wool blend in white

NOTIONS

- Stuffing

HOOK

- B/1 (2.25 mm)

How to Make

1. Crochet each part following the patterns and chart.

2. Stuff the strawberry. Pull the yarn tail to close the opening. Secure and hide the yarn tail.

3. Whipstitch the stem to the leaves.

4. Whipstitch the stem and leaves to the strawberry.

5. Embroider the strawberry with French knots using the white yarn.

Crochet the Strawberry

⬤ = red

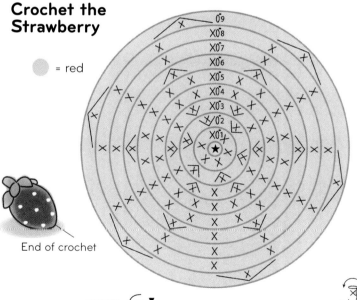

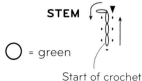

End of crochet

STRAWBERRY

Row	Stitches	
9	6	(-6)
8	12	work even
7	12	work even
6	12	(-6)
5	18	work even
4	18	work even
3	18	(+6 each row)
2	12	(+6 each row)
1	6	skr

STEM

◯ = green

Start of crochet

LEAVES

Use the wrong side of the sc as the outside fabric.

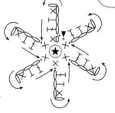

◯ = green

Basket Shown on page 11

Materials

YARN
- 26 yards (6 g) of light fingering-weight (#0 lace) cotton in beige

HOOK
- C/2 (2.75 mm)

How to Make

1. Crochet the basket following the pattern and chart.

Crochet the Basket

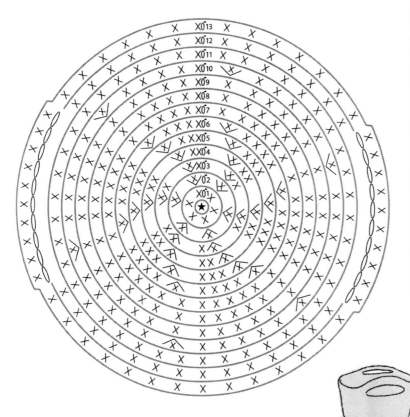

BASKET

Row	Stitches	
13	48	work even
12	48	(+6)
11	42	work even
10	42	(+6)
9	36	
8	36	work even
7	36	
6	36	
5	30	
4	24	(+6 each row)
3	18	
2	12	
1	6	skr

◯ = beige

Life Preserver Ring Shown on page 12

Materials

YARN

- 15 yards (4 g) of sport-weight (#2 fine) acrylic in white
- 15 yards (4 g) of sport-weight (#2 fine) acrylic in red

NOTIONS

- Stuffing

HOOK

- C/2 (2.75 mm)

How to Make

1. Crochet the life preserver ring following the pattern and chart.

2. Stuff. Pull the life preserver ring yarn tails to close the openings. Secure and hide the yarn tails.

Crochet the Life Preserver Ring

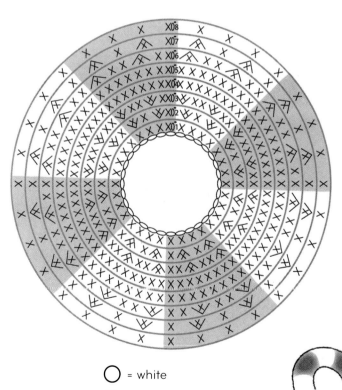

○ = white

● = red

LIFE PRESERVER RING

Row	Stitches	
8	32	work even
7	32	(-16 each row)
6	48	
5	64	work even
4	64	
3	64	(+16 each row)
2	48	
1	32	ch 32

Use white for chain stitch (ch).

Banana

Shown on pages 12–13

Materials

YARN
- 8 yards (2 g) of sport-weight (#2 fine) acrylic in yellow
- 8 yards (2 g) of sport-weight (#2 fine) acrylic in off-white

NOTIONS
- Stuffing

HOOK
- C/2 (2.75 mm)

How to Make

1. Crochet each part following the patterns and charts.

2. Stuff the banana.

3. Whipstitch the banana to the inside of the peel.

Crochet the Peel

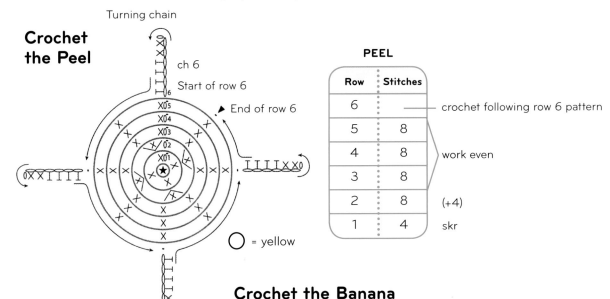

Turning chain

ch 6

Start of row 6

End of row 6

O = yellow

PEEL

Row	Stitches	
6		crochet following row 6 pattern
5	8	
4	8	work even
3	8	
2	8	(+4)
1	4	skr

Crochet the Banana

BANANA

Row	Stitches	
5	6	
4	6	work even
3	6	
2	6	(+2)
1	4	skr

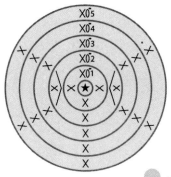

= off-white

Assembly Diagram

BANANA
Row 5 of peel

Watermelon Shown on page 12

Materials

YARN

- 23 yards (6 g) of sport-weight (#2 fine) acrylic in green
- 8 yards (2 g) of sport-weight (#2 fine) acrylic in black

NOTIONS

- Stuffing

HOOK

- C/2 (2.75 mm)

How to Make

1. Crochet the first 12 rows of the watermelon following the pattern and chart.

2. Stuff.

3. Crochet the final row.

4. Embroider the zigzags with backstitch using the black yarn.

Crochet the Watermelon

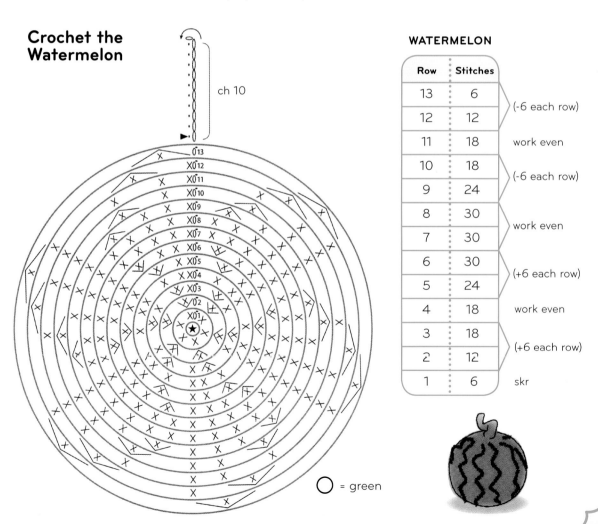

ch 10

○ = green

WATERMELON

Row	Stitches	
13	6	(-6 each row)
12	12	
11	18	work even
10	18	(-6 each row)
9	24	
8	30	work even
7	30	
6	30	(+6 each row)
5	24	
4	18	work even
3	18	(+6 each row)
2	12	
1	6	skr

Red Maple Leaf Shown on pages 18–19

Materials

YARN
• 9 yards (2 g) of fingering-weight (#1 super fine) acrylic/wool blend in red

HOOK
• B/1 (2.25 mm)

How to Make

1. Crochet the leaf following the pattern.

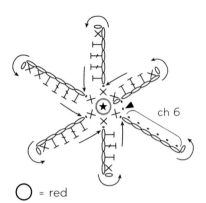

ch 6

◯ = red

Ginkgo Leaf Shown on pages 18–19

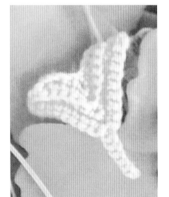

Materials

YARN
• 9 yards (2 g) of fingering-weight (#1 super fine) acrylic/wool blend in yellow

HOOK
• B/1 (2.25 mm)

How to Make

1. Crochet the leaf following the pattern.

2. Join yarn to leaf and crochet stem.

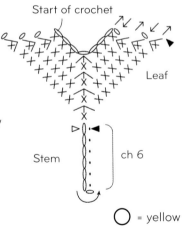

Start of crochet

Leaf

Stem

ch 6

◯ = yellow

Scarf Shown on page 25

Materials

YARN

• 13 yards (3 g) of aran-weight (#4 medium) acrylic/mohair blend in yellow

HOOK

• B/1 (2.25 mm)

How to Make

1. Crochet the scarf following the pattern. Crochet until scarf measures $9\frac{1}{2}$" (24 cm) long.

2. Tie fringe to each end of the scarf.

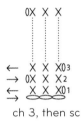

ch 3, then sc

$\bigcirc$ = yellow

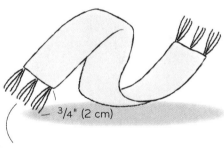

$\frac{3}{4}$" (2 cm)

To make each tassel, tie two $\frac{3}{4}$" (2 cm) long strands of yarn to the scarf. Make three tassels on each end of the scarf.

Acorn Shown on pages 18–19

Materials

YARN

- 8 yards (2 g) of fingering-weight (#1 super fine) wool in reddish brown
- 5 yards (1 g) of fingering-weight (#1 super fine) acrylic/wool blend in beige

NOTIONS

- Stuffing

HOOK

- B/1 (2.25 mm)

How to Make

1. Crochet each part following the patterns and charts.

2. Stuff the acorn. Pull the yarn tail to close the opening. Secure and hide the yarn tail.

3. Whipstitch the stem to the cap, then whipstitch the cap to the acorn.

Crochet the Stem

Start of crochet

◯ = beige

Crochet the Cap

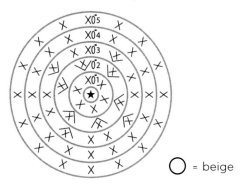

◯ = beige

CAP

Row	Stitches	
5	16	work even
4	16	
3	16	(+4)
2	12	(+6)
1	6	skr

Use the wrong side of the sc as the outside fabric.

Crochet the Acorn

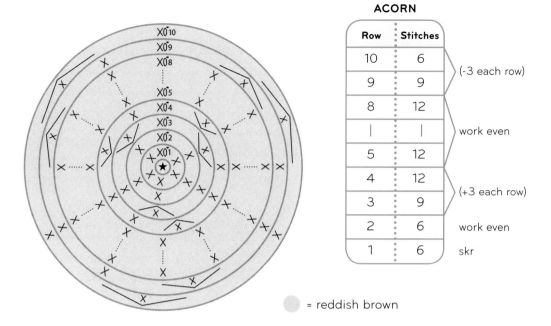

ACORN

Row	Stitches	
10	6	(-3 each row)
9	9	
8	12	
			work even
5	12	
4	12	
3	9	(+3 each row)
2	6	work even
1	6	skr

○ = reddish brown

Assembly Diagram

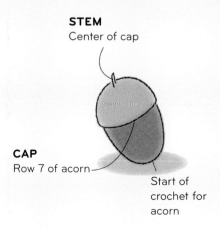

STEM
Center of cap

CAP
Row 7 of acorn

Start of crochet for acorn

Mushroom
Shown on pages 18–19

Materials

YARN
- 18 yards (4 g) of fingering-weight (#1 super fine) acrylic/wool blend in red
- 9 yards (2 g) of fingering-weight (#1 super fine) acrylic/wool blend in beige
- 9 yards (2 g) of fingering-weight (#1 super fine) acrylic/wool blend in white, pink, or yellow

NOTIONS
- Stuffing

HOOK
- B/1 (2.25 mm)

How to Make

1. Crochet each part following the patterns and charts.

2. Stuff the cap and stem.

3. Pull the cap yarn tail to close the opening. Secure and hide the yarn tail.

4. Whipstitch the stem to the cap.

5. Whipstitch the polka dots to the cap.

Crochet the Stem

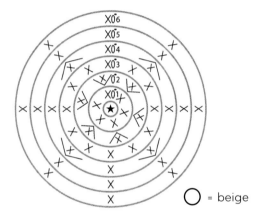

◯ = beige

STEM

Row	Stitches	
6	8	work even
5	8	
4	8	(-4)
3	12	work even
2	12	(+6)
1	6	skr

Crochet the Cap

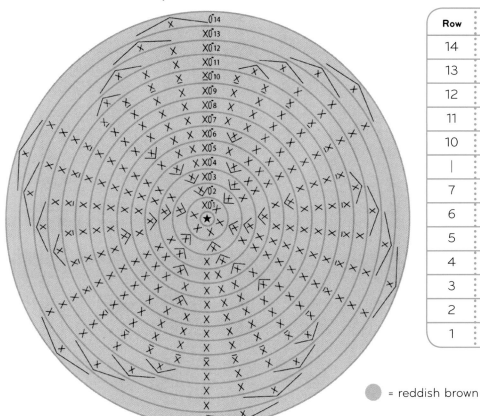

Row	Stitches	
14	6	
13	12	(-6 each row)
12	18	
11	24	
10	30	
|	|	work even
7	30	
6	30	(+6)
5	24	work even
4	24	
3	18	(+6 each row)
2	12	
1	6	skr

CAP

= reddish brown

Crochet the Polka Dots

= white, pink, or yellow

POLKA DOTS
(make 6)

Row	Stitches	
1	6	skr

Use the wrong side of the sc as the outside fabric.

Assembly Diagram

POLKA DOT
Center of cap top

POLKA DOTS
Rows 4-8 of cap (equally space remaining 5)

STEM
Center of cap bottom

View of cap from above

Bears-To-Go Shown on page 28

Materials

YARN

- 26 yards (6 g) of fingering-weight (#1 super fine) acrylic/wool blend in brown, green, or purple
- 9 yards (2 g) of fingering-weight (#1 super fine) acrylic/wool blend in white
- 5 yards (1 g) of fingering-weight (#1 super fine) acrylic/wool blend in black

NOTIONS

- Two 4 mm diameter eyes in black
- Mobile phone strap
- Embroidery floss in black (3 strands)
- Stuffing

HOOK

- B/1 (2.25 mm)

How to Make

1. Crochet each part following the patterns and charts.

2. Stuff the head, body, nose, and snout.

3. Whipstitch the nose to the snout. Embroider the mouth with the embroidery floss.

4. Attach the eyes. Whipstitch the snout and ears to the head.

5. Whipstitch the head to the body.

6. Whipstitch the arms, legs, and tail to the body.

7. Attach the strap to the head.

Crochet the Arms and Legs

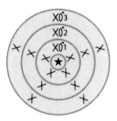

⬤ = brown, green, or purple

ARMS AND LEGS
(make 2 each)

Row	Stitches	
3	5	work even
2	5	
1	5	skr

Crochet the Body

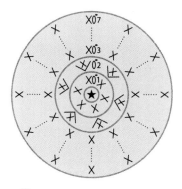

BODY

Row	Stitches	
7	12	
|	|	work even
3	12	
2	12	(+6)
1	6	skr

⬤ = brown, green, or purple

Crochet the Head

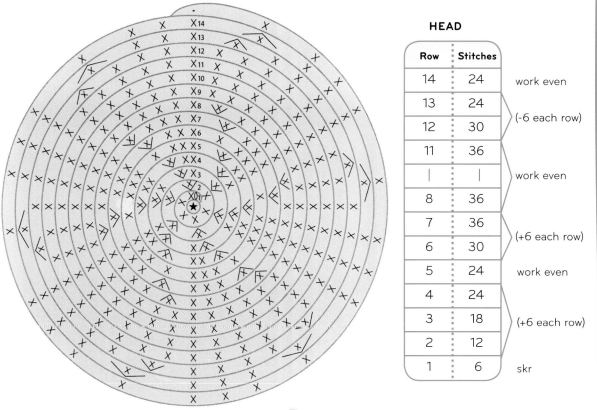

HEAD

Row	Stitches	
14	24	work even
13	24	
12	30	(-6 each row)
11	36	
|	|	work even
8	36	
7	36	
6	30	(+6 each row)
5	24	work even
4	24	
3	18	(+6 each row)
2	12	
1	6	skr

⬤ = brown, green, or purple

Crochet the Ears

⬤ = brown, green, or purple

EARS
(make 2)

Row	Stitches	
4	12	work even
3	12	
2	12	(+6)
1	6	skr

Crochet the Snout

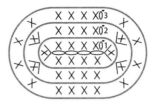

◯ = white

SNOUT
(make 2)

Row	Stitches	
3	16	work even
2	16	(+4)
1	12	ch 4

Use the wrong side of the sc as the outside fabric.

Crochet the Nose

NOSE

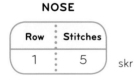

Row	Stitches	
1	5	skr

⬤ = black

Use the wrong side of the sc as the outside fabric.

Crochet the Tail

⬤ = brown, green, or purple

TAIL

Row	Stitches	
1	6	skr

Use the wrong side of the sc as the outside fabric.

Assembly Diagram

EARS
Rows 3-7 of head

HEAD
Start of crochet

EYES
Row 8 of head
(8 stitches between eyes)

Row 2 of snout

Row 1 of snout

Start of crochet for snout

4 stitches

NOSE
Rows 2-3 of snout

SNOUT
Rows 8-12 of head

ARMS
Row 6 of body

LEGS
Rows 2-3 of body

TAIL
Rows 2-4 of body

What else can you create with a crochet hook?
CHECK OUT THESE OTHER SOURCES OF INSPIRATION!

Get hooked with more sources of inspiration at
CrochetMe.com, linking the crochet community

crochetme